# *How to enjoy opera without really trying*

## JOHN CARGHER

HILL OF CONTENT
Melbourne

First published in Australia, 1986
Reprinted 1986

This Australian edition published by
Hill of Content Publishing Co. Pty Ltd
86 Bourke Street, Melbourne 3000 Australia
in association with the
Australian Broadcasting Corporation

© Copyright John Cargher, 1986

Designed by Helen Semmler
Typeset in Australia by
Abb-typesetting Pty Ltd Collingwood, Victoria
Printed by Everbest Printing Co. Ltd. Hong Kong


Cataloguing-in-publication data

Cargher, John.
   How to enjoy opera without really trying.

   Includes index.

   ISBN 0 85572 163 4

   1. Opera. I. Title.

782.1'015

Front cover:
Puccini's *Turandot*, Royal Opera House Covent Garden
Photographer — Zoe Dominic

*How to enjoy opera
without really trying*

# Contents

# CHAPTER ONE

# "The Opera Ain't Over till the Fat Lady Sings!"

*T*hat famous saying may have described the supposed suffering of opera-lovers once upon a time. It does so no more. Opera today is a high-class entertainment which demands good-looking men and shapely girls to act out dramatic stories that are as convincing as any straight play or film.

There is a tremendous boom in opera, though it does not attract the tens of thousands of fans that pop singers do — and never will. Why? Because opera would be lost in the vast spaces needed to accommodate so many people.

What was once the private pleasure of the rich has become re-established among the masses, as it was in the nineteenth century.

This book does not try to tell you what you 'ought to' enjoy, but what people like you actually do enjoy and why you should not miss out.

England used to be described as 'The Land Without Music', because fewer people went to musical events there than in Germany, France or Italy. But the most recent figures at my disposal show that in the 'Land Without Music' nearly $20 million dollars worth of subsidised opera seats were sold in 1984! And the *average price* per ticket was $18. (Without going into complicated mathematics, this means that far more tickets were sold below that price than above.)

*The fat lady ain't fat any more.* Opera is drama (with music) and needs dramatic reality. Warrior maidens who seduce warrior heroes must be seductive to our modern eye, not that of the 19th century.
(*Above: Die Walküre* by Wagner — Staatsoper, Vienna)
(*Opposite:* Blanche Marchesí in *Die Walküre* — Covent Garden 1902)

Fifty thousand people went to see a production of *Die Fledermaus* that year and 49,000 one of *Don Giovanni*, played by a company which did not have one famous star in the cast! And for every ticket sold the government had to provide a subsidy of $40! In other words, for every dollar spent on opera by the public, the government (the tax-payer) had to spend more than two!

If this sounds like something out of *Alice in Wonderland* in times of high unemployment, inflation and all the rest, ask yourself why, in a survey of tax-payers who do *not* go to the opera, 80 per cent said that the millions given to opera is money well spent.

The fact is that opera exists. Opera has not stood still in the ridiculous mouldering elite state, which produced sayings like 'The opera ain't over until the fat lady sings!' No. It is a vital, living art which can offer more than any musical or straight play in a greater variety than any other theatrical presentation. But it is so expensive to stage that it must be subsidised.

In fact, the financial demands on the managements of opera companies are so great because you can't cut corners in opera. You can write a brilliant new play with two characters and one set, or no set at all, and make a fortune. Yet nobody has written an opera for sixty years which will fill a theatre. And nobody will, because composers have stopped writing the kind of music which is the corner-stone on which opera is built. You and I, the ticket-buying public of the late twentieth century, have created a boom for music of a kind which is no longer being written. As a result opera houses have to serve the same works again and again, but in different ways.

Once upon a time the singing was (more or less) all that mattered. If the fat lady sang well, people were satisfied, even if she stood in front of a frayed backdrop of a ridiculous-looking mountain or palace. Today, operas are as up-to-date as the latest television spectacular. Videotapes of operas are selling so well that even inferior productions are snapped up in double quick time. And when even the second-rate moves on the shelves or at the box office, you can be sure of one thing: people want it!

The opera is indeed not over till the lady sings, but she is no longer fat! It is her singing which has multiplied the public for opera a hundredfold or more in the last twenty-five or thirty years. And why? Because the tunes the once-fat lady sang are

"THE

OPERA

AIN'T

OVER

TILL THE

FAT

LADY

SINGS!"

3

HOW TO

ENJOY

OPERA

WITHOUT

REALLY

TRYING

returning to the position they once held close to the top of the Hit Parades! Yes, it is true. A hundred or more years ago the Hit Parade consisted of tunes from the latest operas and it may surprise you to learn that television in the 1980s still uses a lot of those same hits — mostly in the commercials!

Just think about that for a moment. Commercials are aimed at the mass market, at attracting the maximum number of people watching at any given moment. The tune which catches their ear, which makes them look at the product being sold, must be catchy, easily remembered and, most important of all, popular. And if a tune written in 1875 can sell garage doors in 1986, that surely makes it a bigger hit than any of the standards produced by the Beatles or the Rolling Stones.

Modern pop music is rapidly becoming a visual medium. Video clips sell today's songs and promoters of groups spend more money on lights, smoke, fireworks, garish costumes and make-up than amplifiers and microphones, let alone instruments. But opera has been doing that for centuries! No wonder it became the pop music of its time.

What, then, happened to bring this once popular kind of spectacle into disrepute with mass audiences and young people in particular? How and why was it turned into an elite art in which snobbery was more important than entertainment values? To be blunt: opera priced itself out of the market. It happens to be the most expensive form of theatre and every ticket to it ought to cost far more than the $58 average ($18 plus the $40 per seat subsidy) quoted for 1984 by British subsidising bodies — they did not add private sponsorships and other factors which help to keep prices down. In 1985 the public's share of the cost of a ticket at Covent Garden was $80 — before subsidies!

When the best singers can demand and get $15,000 or more for one performance, the sky is the limit for the actual price per ticket which should be charged, but never is. You can be sure of one thing: your share of the cost of any performance of opera which you attend is quite unrelated to the cost of its staging that night, let alone the overheads involved. Any major opera company employs between 400 and 600 people full-time throughout the year and in recent years single productions costing in excess of a million dollars have not been unknown. Without public funding opera would simply die. In some cities this has already happened and the battle for funds is a major item on the agenda of every opera company's board meetings.

In the bad old days the rich snobs, who ruined opera's image in English-speaking countries, gave millions of dollars for the privilege of literally buying their own private boxes in opera houses in perpetuity as a means of showing off their wealth. The music lovers in the gallery were not to know that they used those boxes to sleep in during those boring evenings, were they?

Royalty at least had the excuse that going to the opera was an official duty. English kings and queens, with rare exceptions, did not have to pretend enthusiasm for grand opera. Once, when Edward VII, who preferred actresses to singers (off-stage), attended an official performance, Sir Thomas Beecham asked his private secretary how the monarch had enjoyed the opera. He replied: 'Three quarters of the way through he woke up suddenly and said "Fritz, that's the fourth time that infernal noise has roused me!"'

Nevertheless, royalty attended the opera and that meant that society had to do the same, like it or not. 'Patrons of the arts' were welcome at court and used opera to promote their own self-esteem. Unfortunately, to the daily papers these people were news and the musical illiterates among the upper classes became identified with an art they not only found boring, but by which they were seen to be bored. How were audiences to be increased when going to the opera meant no more than getting your name in the papers?

At the turn of the century even the *Times* (in London or New York) devoted more space to describing the audience, the dresses and the jewellery worn by the ladies than to the music at Covent Garden or the Metropolitan. In the days when official government support was non-existent the aristocracy and the new industrial barons could afford the astronomical prices and donated major sums to support their favourite social pastime. No wonder opera was an elite art and the token payments of the poorer classes up in the gallery meant so little to the management.

The entertainment value of opera was acknowledged and kept alive by minor impresarios, such as the aging eccentric Lilian Baylis, who offered opera and Shakespeare in the Royal Victoria

"THE

OPERA

AIN'T

OVER

TILL THE

FAT

LADY

SINGS!"

HOW TO

ENJOY

OPERA

WITHOUT

REALLY

TRYING

Coffee Hall in South London, which later became the still existing Old Vic Theatre. Miss Baylis' sixpenny tickets proved so popular that she built the Sadler's Wells Theatre with the proceeds! You can be sure the critics gave more space to the opera there than to what was worn in the auditorium of the new theatre, which did not have even one box for private sale!

I have spoken most about England, because its statistics are the most up-to-date. But opera in all countries enjoyed a similar boom. The gold fields of California and Australia demanded — and got — their operas, if not perhaps the same quality which was seen in London but, curiously enough, the same artists and often the same opera companies. The circuit was Europe-U.S.A.-Australia-Europe — unless, as happened far too often, the company manager fled with the takings and left his singers stranded somewhere along the way and, worse, many perished in shipwrecks. What passed for productions in improvised theatres, sometimes in the tent cities of Australian gold fields, can be imagined.

On the Continent opera was much more readily accepted; it was, and still is, a family entertainment. To this day the first seats to be sold are the cheapest seats. Children were and are taken to the opera as a matter of course. Governments and city councils encouraged opera-going with generous subsidies long before England or the U.S.A. belatedly recognised that music-lovers are also voters.

European opera houses get up to 85 per cent of their expenses back from governments, and the most dedicated opera lovers are found in the cheapest seats. In English-speaking countries opera companies have to plead from year to year for funds to keep this most expensive of all the theatrical arts going. And every change of government means a new battle to survive.

Fashion, not music, dictated the various phases through which opera went over the years. When opera was a popular (and relatively cheap) entertainment in the nineteenth century, curves were considered sexy and well-rounded figures went with our grandfathers' ideas of feminine beauty. The slim fashion models who are imitated by women of all ages today are a product of this century, though fat does not appear to have limited the appeal of certain pop singers of all three sexes in our own time.

The highest paid pop singers in days of old were the stars of opera and they earned astronomical fees. With fat in fashion and banquets laid on for them by royalty and private patrons almost nightly, singers became fatter and fatter. Success and fat went together and dramatic realism went out of the window.

Happily, the fat ladies in opera are now rarities and only the greatest voices imprisoned in large bodies due to some glandular condition, not over-eating, are accepted by the people who govern the standard of opera productions today.

If fashion affected the looks of opera — and not even the most fanatical advocate of Caruso and Melba's days wants to go back to that aspect of the productions in which they appeared — the impact of music of any kind on the human mind, and heart, was accepted as the major factor in making opera popular. Nobody could whistle the scenery or the figure of the prima donna, but the long-extinct errand boys used to sing the latest arias and every home had a piano and at least one member of the family who thought that he or she should provide vocal renderings or piano arrangements of the pop music of the time — the tunes from operas.

'In the Mood' was an old Glenn Miller number which is still around. Getting in the mood has been music's job for longer than anybody can remember. When Glenn Miller and his orchestra were the ultimate in pop, our parents got 'groovy' or 'hep' the moment the music started.

Since those days music has become an essential part of daily life. It is inescapable, whether as Muzak in a lift, a passing echo from transistors carried by men and women of all ages or as the background to endless films and television. You can tell with your eyes closed what is happening on TV just by listening to the ever-present music. Where would horror films be without the eerie sounds which anticipate the scream-inducing shocks which follow? And what would film-makers do if they did not have those musical climaxes to which the censors cannot object during the obligatory sex scenes?

Obviously music puts us into the right mood for any situation, if it is used in the right way. In opera it can do even more. It has been proved that a quartet can tell a better tale in five minutes than can half an hour of dialogue in a play or film! More famous

"THE

OPERA

AIN'T

OVER

TILL THE

FAT

LADY

SINGS!"

HOW TO

ENJOY

OPERA

WITHOUT

REALLY

TRYING

people than I have put that proposition and more will be said about this in the following pages.

People argue endlessly about what opera should be called. Is it music or is it theatre, or musical theatre? Historically, music wins first place, for the plays on which a lot of operas are based have been forgotten, while the operas are still being performed. But opera is drama set to music, not music with drama added afterwards.

What made opera the popular entertainment it once was, and is becoming again, was not the music, not the drama, but the scenery! People may have left the theatre humming the tunes, but they bought their tickets to see the spectacle which opera impresarios were providing for them.

Remember, we are discussing a time long before the invention of films, television, radio or even records. The most popular operas were the most spectacular, the ones which had volcanoes erupting, earthquakes, shipwrecks, avalanches, floods, burning cities and magic — the more magic, the better. In fact, the popularity of opera as an entertainment was almost exactly what we are experiencing today in films and popular music: people went to see something they have never seen before — accompanied by music. Then it was a shipwreck; today it is war in outer space. Then it was calling up the devil; today it is an avalanche of monsters of all kinds. Yet then and now the ever-present music set the scene, and it was music with popular appeal.

The only difference between the pop music of 1836 and 1986 is that we know today which tunes have lasted 150 years, while nobody can tell what, if any, of today's music will still be around next month, let alone in the year 2136.

But let us not forget the resemblance between the current opera boom and the familiar pop scene. Spectacle and entertainment are the name of the game in both, and if the singing happens to be good and the tunes as familiar as ever, we are getting double value for our money.

This book is an introduction to opera as a form of entertainment. It may be 'art' or 'artistic', words which I abhor in this context, but it is also plain and simple entertainment for millions, exactly what it was for our ancestors. Perhaps we are more sophisticated today, but our producers and theatres have resources at their disposal way beyond what anyone could have imagined when these works were written.

I have just one aim: to replace the totally false image of opera as an elitist, highbrow plaything for intellectuals. It can be all of that, but it can also be rattling good fun — provided that you are introduced to it through the right works. Unlike pop music, opera comes in a huge variety of different shapes and sizes. The stories that opera tells fall readily into different categories, but they alone cannot give you any idea of what you will see and hear if you should find yourself in an opera house.

Individual tastes differ greatly in music, as they do in food, clothes or simply enjoying yourself. You can have two operas of similar content, one of which you will love at once, while you will hate the other. The main bulk of this book concerns those works which on the balance of probabilities nobody will dislike. Ideally, each and every one of these operas should make you instant converts to the medium. I think I can guarantee that none of them (in a reasonably good production) will bore you or make you want to walk out. With luck, you will enjoy any of them sufficiently to try another and go on from there.

Later in the book you will find summaries of most of the main operas which are staged regularly world-wide. Some of you may go overboard for the modern dissonances of Alban Berg or the baroqueries of Monteverdi. Wagner's music may well sweep you off your feet for an hour or so; unfortunately, the hour is likely to turn into four or even more and that is why none of his operas is recommended for people not as yet tuned in to what, to them, will be a new medium.

Let us be realistic. In spite of what has become known as the 'opera explosion' of recent years, only a small proportion of the world's population regularly visits the opera and the vast majority, especially among the younger generation, has not seen even one such work. I hope none of the latter is put off experimenting with those works which I have not listed as first recommendations. Only you can be the judge of your own taste. As your chef for the duration of the following pages I can only recommend certain dishes. The proof of the pudding is in the eating and since you will be paying the bill, the final choice must be yours.

"THE OPERA AIN'T OVER TILL THE FAT LADY SINGS!"

*Which way is up?* The scenery is as mad as the
plot, but not as tuneful as Donizetti's music.
(*Viva la Mamma* — Volksoper, Vienna)

A Glossary has been provided because it is inevitable that some words and names will find their way into the text which are unfamiliar, especially to younger readers. This is, after all, a book for newcomers to opera.

In dealing with a subject as complex as opera, which usually deals with subjects tied to some book or play or an historical figure who is often distorted beyond recognition through the ignorance of the composer and/or the librettist, it is inevitable that I shall have to refer to people in many walks of life, real and imaginary, whose names may be unfamiliar to you. For example, a hundred years ago Offenbach could write an opera like *Orpheus in the Underworld*, confident that all of his audiences had been taught Greek and Roman mythology in school. Authors who were famous then, but are not now, were household words in those days. Today many names survive solely on the basis of their connection with opera, or their identity is known only to experts in specialised subjects now taught only in our higher places of learning.

I do not expect you in this day and age to know all about Sir Walter Scott or Philip II of Spain or Pluto — the god, not the dog! Nor do I wish to fill pages and pages with explanations about people or beings or things which will add nothing to your enjoyment of the entertainment called opera. Inevitably you will come across unfamiliar names in the text. Not knowing their background will not hinder your understanding of what I am trying to say. One and all can be found in any average encyclopaedia, if the glossary's explanation is too brief.

In this context it is unnecessary to know anything at all about Beaumarchais, but the fact that both *The Barber of Seville* and *The Marriage of Figaro*, two operas composed at different times in different countries, were based on plays written by the same man is surely of interest. There is nothing shameful about ignorance on such matters; too much has been added to human knowledge since the day when Beaumarchais was a household word. If he, and others, mean nothing to you, skip them and don't worry. In this book ignorance can safely be classed as bliss!

"THE

OPERA

AIN'T

OVER

TILL THE

FAT

LADY

SINGS!"

11

# CHAPTER TWO

# *Funny Operas*

*T*here are two ways of making you laugh, or at least smile: comedy pure and simple and unintentional humour such as can, unfortunately, be found in abundance in some things which we now find ridiculous or pretentious, while our ancestors did not. I must be honest and admit that a lot of opera which can still be seen today falls in the latter category. But the same can be said about a lot of other things: plays, films, television and sometimes even stranger art forms: paintings, sculpture, music, books and even — dare I say it? — pop, rock, punk or other forms of mass entertainment.

No matter what it is, if people are trying to be creative, to produce something uniquely their own, the road to heaven and the road to hell are both paved with good intentions. Have you ever noticed the way fashion, to give but one example, always begins with extremes? The mini skirt or the cover-up tent or the indescribable fancies of the latest fashion moguls were all funny-peculiar when they started.

Pop music artists have been notorious in recent years for wearing strange outfits so way out that they make some people laugh quite literally; they have gone to ludicrous extremes. The trouble is that anything new looks or sounds strange and that the strangest often turns into something very worthwhile in the long run — after modification! The parents of your parents hated

*A calf and a half of a half of a calf.* The gold of
the Golden Age of Singing in the 1980s extends
to the sets, scenery and costumes.
(*Faust* by Gounod — Staatsoper, Vienna)

what your parents loved just as much as your own parents rub-
bish the things today's youth admires; my generation thought
Elvis Presley corrupted our children, but our fathers said
crooners were pansies! So also with opera.

Everybody loves a good joke, but this is not the place to
analyse humour. The point, or rather question is: can music
make a joke funnier? This is not a trick question, for the answer is
clearly 'No'. The joke without the music will be just as funny, but
music often adds something which no stand-up comedian can
provide; and somewhere in the telling of a few suitable opera
plots I hope to prove all this.

Opera can be funny, but it can also be fun; there is no end to
the variety of entertainments which pass under the forbidding
banner of 'Opera'. It is, in fact, a constantly changing term.
Various sub-sections are recognised by us today which, it can be
proved historically, will ultimately be known simply as operas.

In order of appearance on the scene, there are operas,
operettas, musical comedies, musicals, revues and the ironically
titled 'rock operas'. None describes an absolutely fixed style of
stage work. The first and last on my list probably sum up the
problem best.

I have already stated that there is an immense variety of
operas. But then, opera has been around a long, long time and I
hope to prove that all these works will at some point of the future
become absorbed under the same heading. The so-called 'rock
opera' is basically a musical using rock-'n-roll style music. It took
off with *Hair* and *Jesus Christ Superstar*, but diversified so quickly
that few works are ever advertised as rock operas, though theatre
people refer to them as such.

The intermediate steps between *opera* and *rock opera* have
already lost their identities. There never have been clearly
defined borders between the different forms of musical theatre.
The reality is that Offenbach's *comic operas* were really intimate
revues which satirised the establishment in musical form. The
*operettas* of Johann Strauss were a theatrical elaboration of the
waltz, which was considered an indecent dance by Victorian
audiences; you could not have a Viennese waltz in a 'proper'
(morally as well as musically) opera. Yet Strauss' music demanded trained operatic voices to give his operettas (little

HOW TO

ENJOY

OPERA

WITHOUT

REALLY

TRYING

operas) their full value. And popular demand, and changing moral values, quickly created a new and acceptable variety of a familiar entertainment.

The instant mass appeal of light opera (operetta) led to the exploitation of comedy by stars without voices to match their comic talents. The result was *musical comedy* in which anything went. After a time people got tired of actors singing without trained voices and when *Oklahoma!* appeared in 1943 the *musical* which could not succeed without good voices was born. I leave it to you to decide what history will call the wild variety of styles from *Jesus Christ Superstar* to *The Rocky Horror Show* or *Cats*. But it is my guess that they will all end up as operas one day! Anyway, body microphones have now been perfected to a point which makes it difficult to tell small voices from large.

And this is how it works, or has worked: the much despised operetta found its way into opera houses in the first half of this century. It is certainly not unusual to see *Die Fledermaus* or *The Merry Widow* following *Rigoletto* or *La Bohème*. The number of first-class musical comedies (first-class in musical terms) was limited, but in recent years quite a few, from *No, No, Nanette* to *Showboat* have been updated and are competing with the later musicals. Revues like *On Your Toes* have been equally successful at the box office.

History has got a little ahead of itself by bringing the musical into the opera house more quickly than its earlier cousins, such as the ones mentioned in the last paragraph. *Kiss Me Kate, Fiddler on the Roof, My Fair Lady* and similar works are already regulars in opera house schedules and their popularity ensures that they will remain there.

No opera house makes a distinction between them and the more traditional operas. *My Fair Lady*, with a non-singing Professor Higgins, is as much an opera today as Wagner's *Die Götterdämmerung*. It may not be too long before *Cats* joins them and then we truly will have pop opera mixed with real opera.

All this, of course, pre-supposes that operettas or musicals which find their way into opera houses will be sung in the language of the audiences. To readers of this book that will be English. The argument works equally well for any other language you may care to substitute for my own. Unfortunately,

*Hot air can be uplifting*, whether it is provided
by politicians or opera singers. And its humour
is funny in any language.
(*L'elisir d'amore* by Donizetti — Metropolitan
Opera, New York)

HOW TO

ENJOY

OPERA

WITHOUT

REALLY

TRYING

the vast majority of popular operas were not written in any one language. We hear a lot about Italian opera and Italian singers, but it may surprise you to learn that Paris was always the opera capital of the world and that Germany has always had more opera houses than Italy. Many of the most popular operas were written by Italians, it is true, but opera has always been an international art. (I shall leave alone the reasons why non-Italian countries often played most or even all their operas in Italian, why the king of Prussia spoke French, why a German composer like Carl Maria von Weber wrote *Oberon* in English and why most of the early twentieth century English operas were performed in German.

The question of opera in English or in the original language is the subject of endless controversy. Since the music of no opera has ever been written before its libretto, composers have always demanded that they be sung in the language of the audience. (They do so even today, no matter what the experts may say to the contrary.) Fashion, musicologists and lazy singers have proved to the satisfaction of the musical snobs that music sounds better if sung to the words for which it was written. This is perfectly true and I would not discourage anyone from enjoying a familiar opera in a foreign language. But, in getting to know a new medium, as opera is to the reader of these lines, it is absolutely essential that the text be clearly understood, especially when comedy is at stake. Composers like Wagner, Verdi, Puccini and others insisted on translations, or wrote operas in languages other than their own. They wanted the words to be understood. That is an historic fact.

However, familiarity breeds content and there are ways of enjoying opera in a foreign language. I do not recommend the 'study' of libretti before going to operas which will be sung in Italian or German or Russian. Read the story by all means, but unless (and until) you are an opera buff, you will not be able to distinguish the finer points which are gained by hearing opera in a language other than your own, and that applies particularly to comic operas. Their music was written to make a funny situation or joke work and an understanding of the text is vital to their full enjoyment.

The invention of 'Surtitles' or 'Supratitles' in the 1980s has given theatre audiences the chance to follow foreign operas, and English ones as well, by having the text or translation projected above the stage, a variation of the sub-titles used in foreign films. Surtitles have been a success and will, I believe, become standard equipment world-wide. Nevertheless, I recommend a weaning on operas in English, if English is your language. You will catch the spirit of dialogue which is sung — of words enhanced by music — much more quickly, even though many singers do not pronounce their words as clearly as they should.

Strange as it may seem, our so-called experts seldom mention that Italian and German singers have also been known to have bad diction. Of course, you can argue that if you don't understand the language it doesn't matter whether the words are clear or not. Composers and librettists alike have been known to complain about this as audiences have, but the subject of voice versus words is one on which everybody has agreed to disagree.

Let us assume for the moment that the words being sung are clearly audible and humorous in intent. No doubt, they fail to be so at times, but the author does want to make his audience laugh.

I think even the most uninterested bystander has heard of *The Barber of Seville*, which was written by a young man only just out of his teens; Gioacchino Rossini was all of twenty-two years of age when he whipped up this delightful trifle in nineteen days! One hundred and seventy years later it is safe to say that no week, and possibly no day, passes which does not see a performance of this opera somewhere in the world. Why?

If I say: because it is a very funny piece of theatre, I would not be telling the truth. *The Barber of Seville* has existed as a play for well over two hundred years, but you will rarely see it performed, except perhaps as a museum piece at the Comédie Française in Paris. The original *Barber* appeals to a minority, while Rossini's is loved by millions.

I can just see the wise guys among my readers saying: 'Here it comes: everybody knows that famous aria with its "Figaro, Figaro, Figaro!" and he'll claim that the music of that makes the opera so famous.' Well, to quote the words of another operatic aria: 'It ain't necessarily so!' Not only ain't it necessarily so, it positively ain't so.

The fact that the aria in question, known as 'Largo al factotum'

19

HOW TO

ENJOY

OPERA

WITHOUT

REALLY

TRYING

(I am the factotum of the town) has been satirised and bastardised and eulogised ever since it first appeared only proves the
point I made in the introduction to the book, that opera contains
pop tunes which are immortal. There is nothing basically funny
about this aria, which is a light-hearted introduction of a very
famous character called Figaro.

There is nothing basically funny about Figaro himself, nor has
anybody ever been known to laugh during his introductory aria,
except perhaps through some non-Rossinian addition. The
strength of the opera called *The Barber of Seville* lies not in the
famous arias it contains, but in that it is a model of how
humorous situations can be made even funnier by the addition
of music.

I am talking about music improving a joke, something which
*The Barber of Seville* does so many times that I am not going to
waste time counting them. But let me give you two examples,
neither of which is attached to any famous tune. And the fact that
they are not is the secret of why this opera, and any good comic
opera, continues to be a success: the music adds something to the
text.

In the first act of *The Barber of Seville* the Count Almaviva,
disguised as a student, serenades the Señorita Rosina at night.
There is nothing funny-haha about any of this, though you may
consider the fact that he has brought a small orchestra to accompany him to be somewhat peculiar. On the other hand, they are
playing a sweet little tune which is unlikely to wake the neigh-
bours who, in eighteenth century Seville, would think the singing
of a serenade outside a lady's window not at all unusual.

Well and good, but the serenade, like all good things, must
come to an end and the musicians be dismissed, while the young
Count follows up his wooing. The joke at this point is on him, for
he miscalculates the payment to the musicians, which is vastly
more generous than they had imagined it would be. They are
absolutely delighted, so delighted, in fact, that they thank him
profusely, much too profusely. He declines their thanks and
sends them away. Or tries to! But, no, this magnificent, munifi-
cent man must be given the credit for his generosity and the
whole neighbourhood is woken by the effusive and extended
thanking which goes on and on and on.

How long such a gag could be carried through in a play is a moot point. The employer of the musicians would surely not be embarrassed for long. But in the opera, Rossini builds one of his famous musical climaxes as the noisier and noisier thanks are heaped on the unhappy suitor's head. The audience laughs, and continues to laugh, for they know full well (from the music) that the poor man's suffering is far from over. What would be a quick chuckle in the play becomes a joke which builds into a belly laugh in the opera.

The second example occurs later in the plot when, due to the complexities of disguises and machinations funny enough in themselves, the police are called to Rosina's house to quell a disturbance. Six people then proceed to tell the sergeant in charge exactly what has happened — all at the same time! In a play they would be stopped at once by the law, but not in this opera. The music makes perfect sense for each of the six different explanations and then juggles them around to create an ever more confusing jumble. This is funny enough by itself, but it is capped by a line which would not have half the impact without Rossini's theatrical flair: the sergeant, having been overwhelmed by an avalanche of sound belted at an ever-increasing tempo by six opera-sized voices, calmly announces: 'I see now!' — and promptly acts exactly as if he has indeed understood every word which has been hurled at him.

In a later chapter I shall explain how similar effects can be obtained in dramatic and even tragic situations. The crux of the matter is that the spoken word is helped by the addition of the music. Not so long ago every good play had incidental music played in the orchestra pit to assist the actors in their work. Many famous composers wrote what is little more than background music of this type. Today it exists only on film and television. Opera is an extension of that principle; even the actors make music — by singing.

A good opera is good from beginning to end. Don't sit and wait for the bits you know; take it as a whole. For example, the whole of *The Barber of Seville* is a delightful farce whose brilliance can hardly be covered by a mere telling of the plot, no matter how detailed. Good as it is, and it is one of the best, its basics have been used many times in other plays and books. Nothing is new

HOW TO

ENJOY

OPERA

WITHOUT

REALLY

TRYING

in spinning a story, it is the telling of it which makes the difference between a good and a bad play, book or opera.


## THE BARBER OF SEVILLE

The basic plot of the opera is simple enough. The Count Almaviva falls in love with young Rosina, who is the ward of the elderly Dr Bartolo. He keeps her locked in his house with the intention of marrying her for her money. Almaviva knows Figaro, the town's barber, who is also the local spreader of news and gossip, doctor, matchmaker, vet, intriguer and whatever else you may cover by the term 'factotum'. Figaro shaves Dr Bartolo every day and is enlisted to get Almaviva into the house to meet Rosina. The various attempts, all doomed to failure, make up the plot of the opera.

Figaro's mind ('Funny thing, how money stimulates the brain!') first has Almaviva disguise himself as a drunken soldier who is billeted on Dr Bartolo. Unfortunately, Bartolo has an exemption in writing from the authorities. The Count is next introduced into the house as a substitute for Don Basilio, Rosina's music teacher, on the grounds that Basilio is ill and cannot give this day's lesson. Unfortunately, Basilio turns up in the middle of the session, but Figaro convinces him that he does indeed have scarlet fever so infectious that only a severe dose of hard cash can cure it — at home in bed, of course.

Inevitably, the lovers give themselves away while they think Bartolo is busy being shaved by Figaro. They decide to elope, while Bartolo expedites his plans to marry Rosina that very night. How Bartolo's own notary marries Rosina to the Count instead of Bartolo makes up the finale of the opera.

Provided that *The Barber of Seville* can be first heard sung in your own language, it is an almost fool-proof introduction to opera. It is full of superb situations exploited expertly for regular laughs and there are at least half a dozen arias and duets which will be familiar to you. Like all the best comedies, it even works when heard in Italian, though the finer comic points are missed.

It is quite a long jump from the first of the Figaro operas,

Rossini's, to the second, which was composed by Mozart. Historically, they were written in the wrong order. Mozart dealt with
Rossini's Almaviva and Rosina after their marriage, but he wrote
his opera thirty years before Rossini produced the story of their
courtship. Both works were based on a series of three plays by
Beaumarchais dealing with the lives of the same set of characters.
Mozart chose to make an opera of the second play and Rossini of
the first. They are not connected musically, though the lives of
the characters can be followed through the dramatic, or comic,
action.

It must be remembered that Mozart belonged to an earlier era
in music. The fact that he is rated higher than Rossini as a composer is not disputed, but the man who wrote *The Marriage of
Figaro* had a profound influence on the history of opera and on
the best ways of treating drama in music. While Mozart may be a
greater composer and *Figaro* superior to *The Barber*, the latter is
by far the better work to introduce a newcomer to the medium.
The musical conventions of Mozart's day, with long passages
of *recitatives* between the arias, are not as readily accepted by
the average person today as the broader humour of Rossini's
music.

This fact makes the need for an understanding of the words
even more important in Mozart's *Figaro*. Before Mozart, music
was not always related to the words it accompanied and even his
best works do not advance the dramatic action as much as the
operas of many lesser, but later, composers. It is much more
likely that you will find Mozart's *Figaro* sung in translation than
Rossini's and that is as it should be.

## THE MARRIAGE OF FIGARO

We left the Count Almaviva married to Dr Bartolo's ward
Rosina. In *The Marriage of Figaro* that match has not exactly turned
sour, but in the seventeenth century marriage was a one-sided
affair; wives were expected to be faithful and husbands were not.
The infamous *droit du seigneur* (which gave the lord of the manor
the right to spend the wedding night with the brides of his
servants) was under attack and Mozart's *Figaro*, while a genuine

HOW TO

ENJOY

OPERA

WITHOUT

REALLY

TRYING

farce in many ways, has a harsh revolutionary undertone; the bride under threat is Susanna, the new Countess Almaviva's maid and she is about to marry our old friend Figaro.

The Count pursues Susanna for his own purposes, while encouraging the coming wedding. The Countess (Rosina) has to deal with a new character, a young boy, Cherubino, who has a crush on her and is bold, young and foolish enough to attempt seduction, even though he is given no encouragement by the Countess. The self-destructing victim of the humour is the Count Almaviva. Cherubino is caught twice in apparently compromising situations with the Countess but in each case escapes with the help of Figaro and Susanna.

While the Count is still trying to claim his *droit du seigneur* with Susanna, that unwilling object of his desire plots his downfall with her employer, the Countess. Together they lure him into the garden at night where, he believes, Susanna will give him what he seeks. However, in the darkness she tricks Almaviva into trying to seduce his own wife, who has switched clothes with Susanna! As for poor Figaro, he is inadvertently fooled into believing that the plot to protect his marital rights is intended to result in the very opposite; but when the Count is publicly exposed in the final scene all is, of course, forgiven.

*The Marriage of Figaro* is a bitter-sweet comedy. If Mozart's music does not have the mischief which Rossini brings to the same characters, it may well be due to the period in which he lived rather than any delicacy of his feelings. Academics and some critics claim to hear pre-echoes of the French Revolution in Mozart's music. This may be the case in the original Beaumarchais play (though this also 'ain't necessarily so') but it is surely making a mountain out of a very small molehill. The composer of *Figaro* was a coarse little man and there is every reason to believe that his opera was intended to be funny in the true sense of the word. The fact that it can be played as a politically motivated drama does not make it any less enjoyable, though its appeal for a newcomer to opera may depend on the producer's whim. It all depends which authority he has read. The historical Mozart would certainly have added laughs by any method he could imagine.

The quickest way to bring home the switch from opera to pop opera can be found through *Die Fledermaus*, probably the earliest operetta to make the transition into the regular opera repertoire, where it now resides in absolute security, waiting to see which of its later cousins will join it and *The Merry Widow* as light-hearted partners for the works of Puccini, Verdi, Wagner and any other 'serious' composer you may care to name.

By an accident of language the practice of translating the title of Johann Strauss' masterpiece has fallen into disuse. Franz Lehár's *The Merry Widow*, the next most popular in line, has never had this problem, because the title covers the plot and music quite adequately. But *The Bat* is as bad a name for the Strauss work as *Die Fledermaus* is for the original German. It is meaningless, except for a few moments of background information not even sung, but spoken by one of the characters. I am not going to try and explain it; it is irrelevant. Consider *Die Fledermaus* as being a German name, a form of identification for the world's most famous pop opera.

Behind the name lurks the most fool-proof theatre piece which has ever been written. There are not many of these — works which will entertain an audience even when shoddily staged, badly sung and amateurishly presented. It has a truly funny plot, which is so simple that it can be understood easily even if sung in German, and music which is the strongest possible argument for sung plays instead of spoken ones. This time it is not a matter, as in *The Barber of Seville*, of jokes being enhanced, but of music which has enchanted millions even without the words. Oddly enough, I am not referring to the Strauss waltzes which abound in *Die Fledermaus*. This opera, operetta or pop opera does not rely on the appeal of its waltzes. The music of such a work must progress its story; the story is complicated and that makes the music complicated. In spite of this, there is not a dull moment from start to finish and even the smallest linking passage brings nothing but pleasure. How? I suppose a couple of examples will once more have to be trotted out.

A husband and wife are forced to part, unwillingly according to the text. Eight days in jail for assaulting a (parking?) inspector.

HOW TO

ENJOY

OPERA

WITHOUT

REALLY

TRYING

One translation begins the farewell with 'Oh dear, oh dear, how sad it is . . .', and so is the music — at first! Then it gradually speeds up and turns into a very fast waltz, as the couple individually remember a reason for the parting which, in each case, is quite different and also, in each case, something very naughty and very pleasant. Joyfully, they dance around the room when suddenly they remember the pretence, the façade they must present to each other, and they revert to bemoaning their lot in the saddest of fashion, while the music reverts to 'Oh dear, oh dear . . .', only to speed up once more, sending both into the night in a turmoil of pleasant anticipation. It simply can't be done with words alone and Johann Strauss was inspired to a degree he was never to equal after *Die Fledermaus*.

Another example: the central ball concerns, like all farces, an attempted seduction, which in this case begins with a chiming pocket watch tuneful enough to catch the eye and ear of any lovely girl with a few glasses of champagne under her belt. The chimes of that watch reappear in various forms throughout that scene without the use of a single word. Once the presence of the watch is established, it needs no further explanation.

*Die Fledermaus*, like most operas, is based on a successful play which, without Strauss' music, is now as dead as the proverbial doornail. It probably included the famous watch, but how often can speaking characters justify its chiming? In the music it adds a piquancy which is irresistible.

*Die Fledermaus* takes place in an operetta never-never land named Vienna in which anything can happen, and does. A middle-aged couple are at home. Rosalinda is preparing her husband, Eisenstein, for his stay in prison. Enter a friend of the family, Dr Falke, who is about to play a practical joke on Eisenstein. He invites him to a ball, suggesting to him that surrendering himself to jail in the morning will do just as well. He also arranges for Rosalinda to be invited and, for good measure, her maid Adele; all three in disguise, of course.

Complications: an old lover of Rosalinda, the tenor Alfred, turns up and, in the absence of the husband, dons his dressing gown and eats the supper he has left. The arrival of the governor of the prison to escort his honoured guest in person to his confinement causes no end of trouble, for he naturally mistakes

Alfred for Eisenstein and, to save a lady's honour, the lover pretends to be the husband and goes to jail for him.

Prince Orlofsky's Ball and some of Strauss' greatest music occupy the second act in which Eisenstein uses the famous watch to seduce a Hungarian Countess (Rosalinda in disguise). Adele makes up to the prison governor (also invited and also in disguise) and Dr Falke plots his revenge as the various fake characters drop their guards in front of others who keep theirs up. The chiming of the watch mixes with the chiming of six o'clock in the morning and there is a tremendous finale in which the principals rush out to meet their various fates.

The final act takes place in the prison where Eisenstein arrives to find that he is already in jail! Was he not arrested the night before in his own home, in his own dressing gown and supping with his wife? In fact, they can hear him singing in his cell at that very moment! There is too much coming and going to make any kind of sense in condensation, but the indignation of Eisenstein is quickly snuffed when he is told in no uncertain terms that last night he was trying to seduce his own wife. The ending is a toast in praise of champagne. *Die Fledermaus* is staged every year on New Year's Eve in both of Vienna's opera houses.

*Die Fledermaus* is a work which is unlike any other. It has to be seen to be believed and heard to be enjoyed. It is living proof that the sound of sung dialogue is not in any way impossibly artificial or silly. This is the work which proves that opera is a valid art form worth every penny you can scrape together for a ticket.


## SATIRE AND REVUE

The last operas to be dissected in the chapter of 'funny' operas may come as something of a surprise. As modern music has become less popular in the classical sense, satire in the theatre and on television or radio has relied less and less on music. I must admit that modern pop music hardly lends itself to humorous treatment. Humour to be effective must be presented in clear English. As far as I can see — and hear — the noise level of rock-'n-roll and its successors is such that any political message contained in the music is necessarily a scream of outrage.

*The Yellow Menace unmasked!* The most
fearful weapon is satire. Offenbach's Chinamen
can be equated with Chaplin's send-up of Hitler
in the film *The Great Dictator*.
(*Ba-ta-clan* by Offenbach — Australian Opera)

I have never heard jokes told, or funny songs sung at the level of decibels present at pop concerts in the 1980s. Yet, making fun of the establishment is still in fashion, and I hope it will never cease to be so. But it is spoken or seen satire. Rarely indeed is it sung and I know of no successful modern musical with political satire as a subject.

This was not always so. Intimate revue, which flourished in the years after World War II, was a throw-back to the comic operas of Gilbert and Sullivan and Offenbach. In England the censor, the Lord Chamberlain, still ruled and when revue numbers were accompanied by music he somehow did not feel the pain so much. Anyway, he was always more lenient with musical send-ups than straight talk, though the subject of political censorship in opera is one worthy of a full-length book by itself.

People love to see their betters humiliated or sent up. It has always been so and the relaxation of censorship has made it easier. The reason why modern musicals from *Hair* onward have concentrated exclusively on *serious* social comment is not clear. But, thanks to the music of Sullivan and Offenbach, the funny side of politics in the nineteenth century is still with us. The trouble is that so many still-popular works fail to leave the kind of impact they once had because the subjects they satirised are no longer with us. Topical satire must be — topical.

The answer has been to update these works and modern producers can stage productions of *The Pirates of Penzance* or *Orpheus in the Underworld* in what some people would call outrageous travesties. They are not travesties in the 1980s any more than updated dramatic operas are travesties. The fact is that jokes only work when the subject of the joke is known to the audience and any comic or funny opera must be updated in words, if not necessarily in music, if it is to succeed today. Fortunately, we have producers of genius who can do this for us.

The heirs of Richard d'Oyly Carte held the sole rights to the Gilbert and Sullivan operas until 1961. The first part of the famous team, W. S. Gilbert, not only wrote the libretti for these works, but produced them for the stage and the d'Oyly Carte family would only allow them to be reproduced as exact copies of the Gilbert original. In the process they nearly succeeded in killing a most enjoyable art form. Now that the copyright has

HOW TO

ENJOY

OPERA

WITHOUT

REALLY

TRYING

expired, the old dears have come back to life and their kick has been so healthy at the box office that opera houses cannot and do not ignore them.

Sullivan wrote rattling good tunes, which most people can and do whistle with ease, but his music was written as an accompaniment to Gilbert's words, not as an extension of them. Obviously, to help the action, there are nice touches by the hundred in the Gilbert and Sullivan operas, but they remain Gilbert and Sullivan, not Sullivan and Gilbert. And it is Gilbert's words which need updating, not Sullivan's music, though the latter is not sacrosanct and can be re-orchestrated at will to back up the spirit of new ideas in our time.

The famous New York production of *The Pirates of Penzance* added musical jokes to Sullivan's score, but they were in the spirit of satire in keeping with what the famous duo were attempting a hundred years ago.

In 1880 Sullivan made fun of Mendelssohn and Gilbert made fun of the London police. In 1981 New York producer Wilford Leach had his Gilbertian hero imitate Elvis Presley! Even so, however much I may approve of what Mr Leach did to *The Pirates*, Gilbert's ideas will ultimately last longer; policemen will be around a long time, but how funny will a Presley imitation be in twenty years' time?

The crux of the matter is that Gilbert and Sullivan do survive and so does Offenbach. Unlike Strauss and Rossini, they require alteration to make them acceptable. Offenbach was an educated man and so was his public. His arrows hit bigger targets than Gilbert's. His operas also were satires of a high order, though he, running his own theatres, never allowed his librettists to get top billing as Sullivan did in London.

In Paris Offenbach sent up the whole court of Napoleon III in *Orpheus in the Underworld* and the might of Prussia in *The Grand Duchess of Gerolstein*. The satirical edge of neither can be duplicated today, because the targets of his arrows are missing. But the old Greek legend of Orpheus and Euridice sent up is as funny as ever and militarism, even nuclear militarism, may yet be hurt by satire, as Hitler was hurt by Charlie Chaplin's film *The Great Dictator*.

Yet in the end we return again and again to the music which

makes these works live, while the satirical plays of the same period are completely forgotten. It is the combination of words with music which makes funny opera live and both Sullivan and Offenbach were geniuses in their field. Produced today with all the resources of modern theatrical techniques, the name of either on the playbill guarantees enjoyment.

# CHAPTER THREE

# *Pop Operas*

*T*here is a big difference between conventional opera and what I would describe as 'pop opera', a form of entertainment which is unrelated to the previously mentioned 'rock operas'. The borderline between pop and popular classics is a vague one, as you will see. Whether the various forms of rock-'n-roll and its successors can survive remains to be seen. Pop tunes like, say, 'Smoke gets in Your Eyes' or 'When the Saints Come Marching In' are already described quite legitimately as classics. They will still be around 150 years from now. But for every pop classic there are many hundreds, even thousands, which have been forgotten. (Whatever happened to 'The Big Apple'? — The dance, not New York City.) Thus, when I refer to pop operas in the coming chapter and later on, I do not mean rock opera. O.K.?

All of the works in the main text of the book are pop operas, the dramatic as well as the comic ones. They are 'pop' as in popular and, on the whole, there are more serious operas which have immediate appeal to the general public than funny ones.

The most famous hit tunes from opera come from the likes of *Rigoletto* or *Carmen* or *Il trovatore*, and I am not only referring to the tunes which became hits in their original form. Many an aria has had new words put to it and entered the 'Top Forty' or whatever the generation of the time may have called the best-selling hits. I remember whistling 'Hear my Song, Violetta', stolen from

HOW TO

ENJOY

OPERA

WITHOUT

REALLY

TRYING

*La traviata* and half of the musical *Kismet*, including 'Stranger in Paradise', comes from Borodin's *Prince Igor*.

And that only touches the tip of the English-speaking iceberg. The Germans in particular 'pop-ularised' half the operas as soon as they were out of copyright. I remember a German hit called *'Wenn du fortgehst von mir'*, which was the 'Prisoners' Chorus' from Verdi's *Nabucco*!

My definition of genuine pop operas is musicals which have found their way into opera houses; and they are multiplying like rabbits. Strangely enough, about half of them are not at all the kind of thing which needs operatic voices. For example, Julie Andrews started life as a soprano, but *My Fair Lady* has little call for such voices, nor did Rex Harrison ever appear in an opera house — though other famous actors have done so. But *My Fair Lady* is one of the pop operas which does have a secure place in opera houses all over the world and may very well become a fully accepted opera in the years to come.

The description 'musical', as opposed to 'musical comedy', is of American origin. The first musical was *Oklahoma!* in 1943. The English equivalent, musical comedy, appeared to die a natural death as soon as the tall, full-blooded, earthy American leading man replaced the small, stylish and very British leading gentleman. The difference between them was not only visual; the Americans expected strong big voices, while the London West End stars were mostly actors with little vocal appeal. Musical comedies could not compete with musicals or operettas when it came to being accepted in an opera house.

The appearance of Stephen Sondheim in America changed the character of the musical, which began to resemble opera more and more. Sondheim's *Sweeney Todd* may be played nightly, but is really is an opera in every sense. You can also quote Gian Carlo Menotti, whose *The Medium* and *The Consul* were staged more than thirty years ago on Broadway and can now be seen only in opera houses.

The Americanism of musicals took a beating in the 1980s, when even America was inundated with a new kind of musical originating in England. Quite possibly the likes of *Evita, Jesus Christ Superstar* or even *Cats* will become accepted as operas one day. Who knows?

*Left, Right, Left, Right;* it does not matter what
your politics are, opera is in tune with either.
Communist writer Bertold Brecht and capitalist
composer Kurt Weill in *The Rise and Fall of the
City of Mahagonny* are more popular today than
in 1931 when the Nazis wrecked theatres
showing it.
(*Aufstieg und Fall der Stadt Mahagonny* by Kurt
Weill — Volksoper, Vienna)

HOW TO

ENJOY

OPERA

WITHOUT

REALLY

TRYING

This is the only pop opera which is universally accepted as an opera proper without my preliminary 'pop.' George Gershwin is not generally considered to be a 'serious' composer, but he wanted *Porgy and Bess* to be called an opera and it was and is staged as such. But no more so than many other works which followed it and made no such claim. It can be quite legitimately argued that the reason why *Porgy and Bess* was not a huge success when it was first produced in 1935 was because its creator insisted on the label 'opera' which then, as now, seems to frighten some people to death.

*Porgy and Bess* was and is one of the best American musicals there has ever been. Its music entered the pop music scene years ago and no vocalist hesitates to sing 'Summertime' or 'It ain't necessarily so' or 'I got plenty of nuttin' in any style which takes his or her fancy. The basics of the work from which these numbers come are the basics of any average musical or opera: a story with spoken dialogue interspersed with songs which carry the story along. Only one criterion would disqualify such a work: if the removal of the songs would leave a play unable to stand on its own feet. The music must advance the action. It is this one thing which makes musical theatre a different thing from ordinary plays with incidental music.

The trouble which haunts Gershwin's only opera is the nature of the libretto, which presents American blacks as inferior to whites. Gershwin was no racist and in 1935 portraying blacks as real people with human feelings was a positive step forward for racial tolerance. Yet we have come so far in the meantime that the good intentions of the libretto are now a liability. Only Gershwin's music keeps it alive and the fact that the work is being staged by all-black companies in America is an indication that perhaps people are beginning to understand the genuine feeling for the underdog on which *Porgy and Bess* is built.

Porgy is a cripple who wheels himself around in a home-built push-cart in Catfish Row, Charleston, South Carolina, U.S.A. — the place is fully spelt out in detail! Bess is the girl of a huge bruiser of a stevedore called Crown, a hard-drinking gambling man who kills someone in a fight. Having to flee, he tells Bess to find herself another (temporary) protector, but he'll be back! Sporting Life, a dope pedlar, offers to take her to New York, but she wants no part of him. In the end Porgy offers her sanctuary in his cellar.

There is an abundance of minor characters and comic as well as serious business, but Bess falls for the kindness of the crippled Porgy after the brutality of Crown. During a violent storm Crown does return to claim Bess and Porgy kills him. But the other inhabitants of Catfish Row are only too happy to have Crown put away and nobody will point the finger at Porgy, though he is taken by the police for interrogation. During his absence Sporting Life convinces Bess that Porgy will be found guilty of the murder and she goes to New York with him. But Porgy comes back with presents for everybody, including Bess — who has gone. The opera ends with Porgy on his little push-cart setting out to find his woman in far-off New York.

In spite of the depressing subject, *Porgy and Bess* is full of life and laughter and rattling good tunes, which were written to be sung by rich heavy voices. An 'acting' *Porgy and Bess* can be made to work, but a properly sung one is more deeply touching. Except for the basic interpretation of blacks as ignorant poor people, it fits well into the 1980s and the music has already become a classic in both the pop and the serious music field. You can hear it sung in nightclubs, open air stadiums or opera houses, or played in orchestral suites in the concert hall. If you want a genuine pop opera, this is it.


### FIDDLER ON THE ROOF

If ever proof were needed that opera can bridge all frontiers, this pop opera is the perfect example. Music without words knows no frontiers. Music with words must be translated. I doubt whether Jerry Bock's *Fiddler on the Roof* was the first modern musical to find its way into an opera house, but the production at the Komische Oper in East Berlin in 1971, only seven years after its Broadway première, made news world-wide, mostly because its producer, Walter Felsenstein, was a genius. The very fact that an East German opera house dared to present a basically anti-

37

*'Dance, singer, dance!'* Many prima donnas
have to dance very well (see Page 40), but
every opera company has its dancers, because
operettas and musicals of all types are standard
fare in opera houses world-wide today.
Sutherland danced in this *Merry Widow*, but
not in the Can-can.
(*The Merry Widow* by Lehár — Australian
Opera)

Russian subject with Jewish emigration as the central theme is remarkable and one of the signs that modern man can accept artistic licence even if it happens not to suit him politically.

There is little justification for bringing this particular work into any opera house, for it really has no singing parts at all. *Fiddler on the Roof* is excellent musical theatre, but operatic voices it doesn't need, as Tevye might put it. And Tevye himself, the only major singing rôle, has been played by all sorts of non-singers, usually Jewish comedians; Zero Mostel was the first, and anything less like an opera singer it would be hard to imagine.

Like *Porgy and Bess*, *Fiddler on the Roof* is a bitter-sweet work. There are no belly laughs, for the subject is tragic, but opportunities to smile are ample. In the small village of Anatevka in Tsarist Russia lives Tevye, the milkman, with his wife and five daughters. Marrying off one daughter is hard enough for a poor man, marrying off five is almost impossible, especially when each and every one of them wants to marry the man of her own choice, an unheard-of thing in an orthodox Jewish community.

The situation is complicated by the regular pogroms against the Jews which are the policy of the Russian government in Tsarist times. To avoid bloodshed a kindly officer warns Tevye of the coming events, but one of Tevye's new sons-in-law is a revolutionary and is sent to Siberia. Hodel, his wife, decides to join him there. And then the worst comes to the worst and the whole village has to be vacated and its inhabitants drift off to Palestine, America or God-only-knows-where.

It is all very depressing, but true to history. The action is the kind of thing which still happens to millions of people inside and outside Russia. The Jewish wedding and customs will be loved by Jewish audiences and will fascinate the Gentile. The tunes are catchy and many are world-famous; 'If I Were a Rich Man' has almost become a household word. *Fiddler on the Roof* is very much pop opera.

## WEST SIDE STORY

It is difficult to know what to include and what to leave out in this chapter, so many modern musicals are being played in opera

HOW TO

ENJOY

OPERA

WITHOUT

REALLY

TRYING

houses these days. *West Side Story* should be the last work to be so honoured, because it is as much a dancing as a singing stage production. On the other hand, most good opera houses have some very good dancers on their payroll.

The composer was the young Leonard Bernstein and the music of *West Side Story* is probably the best known of all the modern works knocking on the opera door for admittance. Once more, the songs are in the repertoire of every pop and cabaret singer, yet they are wonderfully improved by full-blooded singing such as only trained voices can provide. (Even so, the complete recording conducted by Bernstein himself in 1985 with top opera stars does not work as well as some of the actor-singer-dancers who have recorded the music after playing the parts.)

The story is that of Romeo and Juliet transposed into Manhattan's Puerto Rican quarter. The Capulets and Montagues are transformed into street gangs, the Jets and the Sharks. Juliet's balcony is the fire-escape of a tenement. It has been written: 'Truth to tell, *West Side Story* is more of an opera than a musical play . . . better suited for the opera house than the Broadway stage.' I can add nothing to that.

## CANDIDE

This is a ring-in, which is unlikely to be familiar to the majority of my readers, yet *Candide* has been around for thirty years in many different forms and has a cult following to which I also belong. *Candide* is the perfect pop opera and, I am confident, will be around for many, many years. Probably for as long as musical theatre still exists.

This is above all a work in which words, action and music carry an equal burden. It is tuneful, clever and does not sag. The music by Leonard Bernstein, written a year before *West Side Story*, is uniquely its own and has *not* found its way into the repertoire of pop vocalists, though it is eminently suitable for it. The story and its original author, one François Marie Arouet Voltaire, seem to have frightened the horses at the box office. Voltaire was a major historical figure and a French one at that. How could anything by Voltaire possibly be popular entertainment? Or so the argument goes.

Bernstein has revised *Candide* a number of times and several versions have had substantial successes, yet it has never attained the fame or the popularity of other much less worthy pieces of music theatre. It can only be said in all truth that *Candide* is being revived regularly and does appear to have become popular in some opera houses. I include it here, because it is the only work I know which truly fills the bill in every way as the bridge between traditional opera and modern pop opera, provided that it is produced with imagination and acted as well as sung to perfection.

The story is complicated, but belongs to the literary classics in the *Don Quixote*, or *Gulliver's Travels* league. *Candide*, though created in the seventeenth century, is the modern pop equivalent of both of these. He is a pure innocent who, under the tutelage of one Dr Pangloss, firmly believes that everything is done to create the best of all possible worlds. Candide and his beloved, Cunegonde, in a long series of very short adventures pass through every misfortune which life can bring with the greatest possible good humour. The whole thing is so flexible that producers can do almost anything with it. (One staged a long-running production of *Candide* in New York by tearing the complete interior out of a theatre and seating the audience on scaffolding attached to the walls!)

There is not a dull moment from end to end and only very rarely does romance or sadness interrupt a total spirit of fun. *Candide* is modern; it was probably too far ahead of its time in 1956 to be the success it should have been then. Audiences of the 1980s should be and are ready for it. Perhaps it should be cast with Woody Allen or Gene Wilder, whether they can sing or not! I know of no show which offers murder, rape and pillage mixed with laughter and fine music without ever giving offence. Admittedly, it contains no rock-'n-roll, but I bet *Candide* is still around when rock has died a natural death.

## KISS ME, KATE

My last piece of pop opera never ceases to puzzle me. In the first place, it is a work by Cole Porter in which words and music were written by the one man and it relies extensively on vocal and

HOW TO

ENJOY

OPERA

WITHOUT

REALLY

TRYING

musical punning. I would have thought that *Kiss Me, Kate* would not work in translation. Yet it was one of the first American musicals to be staged in Germany, Austria and even Poland and is a tremendous success all over the Continent. Partly this may be due to the fact that it has three leading rôles which need really big voices and if you can find opera singers who can act, their impact is tremendous. And Germany is the country which pioneered acting in opera.

Again, the story is American, though Shakespeare's *The Taming of the Shrew* is its foundation. Two famous actors, once married but now divorced, are working together in a production of the *Shrew*. They remember the good times they have had, including even a venture into operetta; 'Wunderbar' could have been written by Lehár instead of Cole Porter! There is a pair of young lovers, who play the secondary leads. The boy gets involved with some gangsters after losing a lot of money shooting craps.

In the meantime Shakespeare's play has to take its course and the back-stage shenanigans, gangsters included, parallel the action of the play. This again is high farce with jokes playing fast and loose with top notes. *Kiss Me, Kate* is great entertainment and strong proof that pop opera can be made to work in a regular opera company.

# CHAPTER FOUR

# *Thrillers and Chillers*

*T*he two extremes of popular entertainment have the same effect on the listener or viewer, a loss of emotional and some-times even physical control. You can laugh uncontrollably until your stomach aches or you may cower with terror and cover your eyes. The third, middle, alternative is getting involved to the point of tears.

Nobody has ever been able to find out why people love to cry at a film or stand and gawp at gruesome accidents or murders. And the mechanics of laughter are as such much a mystery today as they have ever been. The impact of all three in a darkened cinema is inevitably greater than it can ever be in a seat far from the stage of a live theatre. Films and television can stage a murder or rape much more effectively than live actors in a theatre, unless the words and action are part of an opera. There the picture changes rapidly.

To re-state the principle: opera is a play with music and a very large proportion of the most popular operas are adaptations of popular plays of their time. Often the original play by some very famous author is completely forgotten, but every time *Rigoletto* or *La traviata* or *Faust* is revived, we are reminded that Victor Hugo, Alexandre Dumas and Johann Wolfgang von Goethe wrote plays as well as books. They and nobody else inspired the three operas I have mentioned and their subjects were as horrifying to

*One man and two black widows.* Nothing is
spared when it comes to startling our
audiences today.
(*Le Grand macabre* by Ligeti — English National
Opera, London)

their audiences as any modern horror film is to us. Television in particular has taken the novelty out of the tragic, the horrific, the immoral or the humorous which affected our ancestors so very much. You have to go to the opera to recapture some of that thrill of old. Still, I must admit that in some instances our ideas have changed to such an extent that the once horrific can only bring indulgent smiles, if not outright laughter, today. The fact that operas containing things like that retain their entertainment value in spite of all should give us pause for thought.

Thrills and chills have always played a large part in opera. As in the case of political satire, censors were less likely to be offended by murder set to music than murder most foul by itself. Many a composer chose the most lurid melodramas to set to music to cash in on the public's craving for sensationalism. Few such works survive, except for occasional revivals which are staged for their curiosity value. You may take it that nothing which has been seen in films or television has not at some stage appeared in operas. Every example of human, inhuman or supernatural phenomena can be found set to music.

What follows is no exercise in listing the most sensational aspects of opera, but an attempt to convince you that the principle of human or other monsters set to music can be as entertaining as anything which Hollywood can produce.

Toward the end of the nineteenth century there was a movement in opera composition which the Italians called *verismo*. You can translate this roughly as 'truthfulness to life'. Operas up to that time had been largely concerned with history and fiction about history. Contemporary subjects were frowned on; what people had done a hundred years before did not matter, but theatre patrons could not face up to the reality of life. Murder, rape, treachery and any other kind of mayhem may have occurred every day, but in those days people did not want to see their own frailties reflected on stage.

Not so many years ago modern writers started producing plays which were lumped together as 'school of kitchen sink', because they dealt with working class people and what they did in their kitchens and bedrooms. The kitchen sink dramas of the 1950s are a close parallel to the *verismo* movement in opera.

Unfortunately, the daily lives of people, rich or poor, are

HOW TO

ENJOY

OPERA

WITHOUT

REALLY

TRYING

interesting only if they get involved with extraordinary events. It has been proved more than once that books, plays or films — or operas — about boring people are boring! Who wants to pay money to be bored? Thus *verismo* turned out to be truthfulness about contemporary people who did abnormal things, bad things. Newspapers are full of scandals, murders and swindles, because good news is not news, while bad news sells papers. The same thing has always applied to the theatre or any other kind of entertainment. We want to see something we would not normally see, and it had better be either funny, or tragic, or horrific — or sex.

I hope I have proved in an earlier chapter that comedy can be enhanced by music. That it can improve drama is more obvious; witness the background music which accompanies every film you see. Yet combining music with contemporary happenings among the lower classes was something quite revolutionary in 1890, when *verismo* was first thought of. The fact that *verismo* operas were as unreal as anything which had been done before, or would be done thereafter, is irrelevant. It did start a new kind of opera and my first example of it is probably the best introduction to 'music drama', which is what opera ideally should be.

Two short operas *Cavalleria Rusticana* and *Pagliacci* are usually performed together and have come to be known as 'the immortal twins'. They were written by different composers two years apart, but their box office appeal as a double-bill has never waned and, by the look of it, never will.

The success of *Cavalleria Rusticana* and *Pagliacci* among those who are, in their opinion, incapable of appreciating the finer things in life, is deeply resented by musical snobs. Any opera which has, as both of these have, been played in variety bills in music halls cannot possibly be good music according to the academics. Their composers were condemned for actually conducting their work in such surroundings. The fact that Diaghilev's *Ballets Russes*, which is still regarded as the ultimate in artistic endeavour, played in the same theatre, between clowns and performing seals, makes no difference to these snobs! After all, 'fancy dancing', as ballet used to be known, was an 'inferior' art and if its public liked the music of Mascagni (*Cavalleria*) or Leoncavallo (*Pagliacci*) then they could not possibly be considered

*Not the Song, but the Dance of the Seven Veils.* This is not the reason why *Salome* was banned for years. She later kisses a severed head on the mouth!
(*Salome* by Richard Strauss — Metropolitan Opera, New York)

HOW TO

ENJOY

OPERA

WITHOUT

REALLY

TRYING

seriously as composers. In what way the quality of music can vary according to the venue in which it is played I have never been able to understand.

Snobbery probably plays a large part in all this. 'Classical' or 'serious' music is supposed to be good for us. Good for what? Good for our soul, but not for the pleasure it might give us? Is music a kind of religion or is it an entertainment? I say it is the latter and I am abused for this. But I still enjoy my opera and I believe you can enjoy it too, and the 'immortal twins' are a perfect example of what I am talking about, for they meet all the specifications of what opera is all about.

The common factors between the two operas are many. Neither contains any spoken words or *recitative* (half-sung linking dialogue between arias) at all or even set arias of any kind. From beginning to end both operas are stories told completely in music. You have probably heard bits and pieces from each; they contain so much music of immediate tunefulness that both vocal and instrumental selections from these two operas have always abounded. In the theatre, these extracts have no beginning or end; they are part of a continuous whole and far more effective for all that.

Consider the most famous extract of all, 'Vesti la giubba' ('On with the motley') from *Pagliacci*. It is the emotional climax of a long scene in which an actor in a travelling show has discovered that his wife is unfaithful to him, and he is faced with going on to a stage to perform (with her) in a play in which he will be the figure of fun, a cuckolded husband!

'The people pay you and want their laugh!' 'The show must go on!' — and all those, by now old, show-business clichés. The famous aria, as sung separately by every tenor who was ever good enough to stand before a willing, or unwilling, audience, must end with the final sung notes, which are not even very spec-tacular or musically complete. In the opera they are followed by a minute and a half of music during which the despairing man staggers off the stage to meet his fate in the next act. The set piece we all know is no more than the central part of a long scene which makes admirable dramatic sense. It was never intended to be sung as a separate item.

*Pagliacci* is probably as close to what *verismo* was intended to be as anything will ever be — a play with music about real people. And so is *Cavalleria Rusticana*. Both operas are set in Italian villages. In some productions they are actually placed in the same village. *Cavalleria* is closer to 'kitchen sink' than *Pagliacci*, because it is a genuine piece of life in such a village. The action of *Cavalleria* is the kind of thing which happened every other day in Italy in Mascagni's time and is probably happening every other week today.

## CAVALLERIA RUSTICANA AND PAGLIACCI

In a small Italian village Turiddu is the local Romeo who seduces every girl in sight. Santuzza is one of his innocent victims, hopelessly in love with him. Now she finds herself cruelly and finally discarded. She is not even pregnant; the loss of her virginity is enough to condemn her in this community. Right now Turiddu is after easier prey, a married woman. Lola is the wife of Alfio, whose business takes him away from the village a lot. The frustrated Santuzza betrays the lovers to Alfio, who takes the only honourable way to avenge himself. He duels with Turiddu in a fair fight and Turiddu is killed. Rustic chivalry — that is the translation of *Cavalleria Rusticana*.

Not much of a story and there is not even the thrill of a duel — that takes place off-stage. But Mascagni's music, from the first notes of dawn breaking over the village, hits you right between the eyes, or ears. You don't have to wait for arias here; the musical action never stops and the highlight of the Easter Hymn, sung while the villagers go to church, is the most fool-proof audience pleaser ever written by any composer. The fact that the actors in this drama do not speak, but sing, is assimilated before the action even commences, when we hear Turiddu serenading Lola in the distance. The first half of this double-bill convinces most people of the potential enjoyment to be gained from opera. The hair-raising end of the second seals the newcomer's fate.

*Pagliacci* has everything a good opera should have, from the famous Prologue which is sung in front of the curtain at the start. In five minutes of music and a limited number of words Leoncavallo summarises the life of every actor on any stage: 'We are

49

HOW TO

ENJOY

OPERA

WITHOUT

REALLY

TRYING

but men like you', with the same problems and feelings. This composer wrote his own words. Greater music may have been written in academic terms, but *Pagliacci* is the perfect wedding of words and music to create music drama, the model all composers should follow. To top it all off, it has almost as many tunes as *Cavalleria* and a dramatic situation which leaves its partner standing at the post. *Pagliacci* is a thriller, and a good one!

Canio and Nedda are the leaders of a travelling group of players. The husband is a violent, jealous type and the wife a light-hearted flirt who wants to better herself in life. Their two companions are the cripple Tonio and young Beppe. Beppe is the romantic lead in a farce in which Nedda plays the wife of a drunk, cuckolded clown of a husband. Tonio provides the light relief as a comic servant in love with the fickle wife.

The play, which is staged in full during the opera, is too close for comfort to real life, except that it is not Beppe who is Nedda's lover, but Silvio, one of the villagers. Otherwise their real lives parallel the play exactly. Before the performance, Tonio declares his love for Nedda. She rejects him, cruelly taunting him for his ugliness. In revenge, Tonio exposes the lovers to Canio, who chases, but fails to catch, his wife's lover.

And thus the play begins that night and every word spoken is an echo of what Canio knows to be the truth about his own life. Goaded on by his stage wife, he refuses to stay in character. 'No, Pagliaccio no more' he sings and demands the name of Nedda's lover. The fight which follows delights the audience, who applaud the admirable acting. Canio stabs Nedda and she calls Silvio with her dying breath. Silvio also is killed and the stunned audiences (on stage and in the theatre) are faced with what has become a classic line: '*La commedia è finita*' — the comedy is ended.

Ended indeed! The play-within-the-play is sung throughout and I defy anybody not to be shattered by a good performance of it, or even a bad one!

## RIGOLETTO

This opera also, if in a different way, was a milestone in the history of opera. It marked the turning point at which Giuseppe

Verdi showed the way to linking the music of a full-length opera without breaks, in which every minute advances the action musically as well as dramatically. Before *Rigoletto* in 1851 operas still consisted of set arias linked by musical bridges which were little more than fillers.

Verdi became Italy's most famous composer because he roused audiences to a frenzy with his sweeping tunes, many of which had political overtones in a country which was still largely occupied by foreign powers; there was to be no Italy as such for another decade or so.

The story of *Rigoletto* came from a play by Victor Hugo and represented the kind of blood and thunder stuff so popular during the nineteenth century. The music which has kept it alive as Verdi's most popular opera has some of the cohesiveness of *Pagliacci* and is for long periods vastly superior to it, though it is not as consistent. So famous is *Rigoletto* and so popular that people forget that the rousing tunes of Verdi's earlier works still break into the action at the most unexpected and even inappropriate moments. When Gilda dies in her father's arms, he launches into a glorious melody which could be attached to almost any other sentiment. It is the greatness of Verdi and of *Rigoletto* that by then, at the very end of the evening, that same tune becomes a heart-breaking lament because of the continuity and dramatic development of the story to this point.

This opera also contains a famous quartet which is one of the strongest arguments for the superiority of opera over straight drama — the composer's ability to have several characters develop separate story lines simultaneously. Victor Hugo himself resented the popularity of *Rigoletto*, because it completely eclipsed his play on which it was based, *Le Roi s'amuse*. But when he heard this quartet, he exclaimed: 'If I could make four characters in my plays speak at the same time, and have the audience grasp the words and sentiments, I would obtain the very same effect.' The fact that, no matter how hard he tried, he did not succeed, did not lessen his enthusiasm for *Rigoletto* from that day on. I shall return to the famous quartet in a moment.

Opera invariably simplifies plots, because it takes much longer to sing words than to speak them, though more can be said through the music than through the text. Thus adaptations of

HOW TO

ENJOY

OPERA

WITHOUT

REALLY

TRYING

existing plays, as happened in this case, invariably reduce the number of principals to a minimum. Lesser figures simply fall by the wayside. There are only three major characters in *Rigoletto*, though three others play minor key rôles. Rigoletto is the hunchbacked jester at the court of the Duke of Mantua in the sixteenth century. The Duke is a typical libertine of his time, all-powerful and inclined to help himself to any woman within reach. Those who affect the story line are the never-seen daughter of Count Monterone, the Countess Ceprano, Maddalena, the sister of the cut-throat Sparafucile and, last but not least, Rigoletto's own daughter Gilda.

Monterone complains about the seduction of his daughter and is punished by the Duke with imprisonment and ultimately death. The Countess Ceprano appears only briefly, about to give in to the Duke's seduction. She and her husband make it clear that they are part of a pleasure-loving court at which anything goes. Seduction of wives, daughters and anything in skirts is the rule of the day. The ruination of Monterone's daughter occurs before the opera starts. His imprisonment and execution for protesting at the fact are the motivation which starts and ends the opera, with the brief, but important and tuneful, intervention of Maddalena, who is seen only during a few minutes in the last act. Minor characters, Monterone and Maddalena, begin and end the tragedy.

When Monterone is imprisoned, the jester Rigoletto sits in judgement on him and mocks his misery. Monterone retaliates by placing 'a father's curse' on him. What follows is the fulfilment of that curse.

In the meantime the Duke has met Gilda while disguised as a student. There is a farcical, but far from funny, scene in Rigoletto's house involving Gilda, her governess, Rigoletto, the Duke and the courtiers, which ends in the abduction of Gilda by the henchmen. They present her to the Duke under the impression that she is Rigoletto's mistress. When the Duke suddenly finds Gilda in his own palace, he promptly seduces her. She pleads sorrow to her furious father, who vows vengeance on the Duke. Rigoletto hires the assassin Sparafucile to kill the Duke.

The last act takes place in the house of Sparafucile in the

country. This brings the famous quartet into the picture. The participants and their rôles in this are as follows: inside the house the Duke is up to his old tricks, this time making love to Maddalena, Sparafucile's sister. Outside in the street are Rigoletto and Gilda. He gloats over the impending doom of the Duke, she is madly in love with her seducer and ready to save him by sacrificing her own life. All this in the span of one four-minute quartet!

A storm brews up — one of Verdi's most inspired creations — and Gilda returns, disguised as a man. Maddalena, who is in love with the Duke, prevails upon her brother for clemency. She lets the Duke escape, while Sparafucile opens the door to an apparently casual traveller (Gilda) and stabs her. Her body is put in a sack and delivered to Rigoletto for the agreed twenty ducats. There follows the kind of masterstroke which has made *Rigoletto* immortal: Rigoletto is about to throw what he believes to be the Duke's body into the river when he hears what is unmistakably the Duke singing in the distance. He opens the sack, finds his own daughter and watches her die. Monterone's curse has been fulfilled.

The music of *Rigoletto* is world-famous, the arias and ensembles too numerous to list here. It is an opera in four short acts without a dull moment musically or dramatically.

## CARMEN

The most performed, most filmed and most bastardised opera of all is *Carmen* by Georges Bizet. The 'bastardised' part of that first sentence is not intended to be in any way derogatory; it is simply a fact that the music of Carmen has been used in endless suites, variations, arrangements and ballets, from symphonic proportions to solo violin pieces. It is an absolute impossibility for any European or American not to know at least some of the music from *Carmen*, or at least the film *Carmen Jones*, which was straight Bizet jazzed up just a little.

What catches the public eye about *Carmen* rather than some other opera is hard to establish. So popular has this opera been

53

HOW TO

ENJOY

OPERA

WITHOUT

REALLY

TRYING

that it has changed the world's concept of Spanish music. *Carmen* is a French opera and its tunes are not genuine Spanish music, but the kind of music which a Frenchman in 1874 believed to be Spanish. Its most famous aria, the 'Habanera' is not an aria at all, but a song by Sebastián Yradier called 'El arreglito'. Curiously enough, stage and film productions which don't use Bizet's music are common; the very name *Carmen* has such a box office pull that unscrupulous producers have tried to cash in on it on many occasions. Even Charles Chaplin made a silent film of it and Geraldine Farrar, who sang Carmen opposite Caruso, made another just as silent! The number of sound films in more recent years is incalculable.

While the music indubitably is responsible for the lasting fame of the opera, its story and dramatic content give tremendous power to good interpreters and original directors. Its flexibility has some bearing on this. It was written originally with spoken dialogue between the musical numbers, but after Bizet's death the spoken parts were set to music and this version is more commonly heard these days.

Carmen is a very modern miss; she works in a cigarette factory! If the subject of *Rigoletto* is a father's curse, that of *Carmen* is fate. The 'Fate Theme' recurs throughout and the amoral character of Carmen herself is based entirely on fate taking her wherever it wishes. It begins with her meeting Don José, an army corporal in Seville, who helps her to escape arrest. After serving a sentence for this, he follows her to a dingy tavern where their affair is consummated after the introduction of Escamillo, the famous Toreador. (It should have been a *matador* — *toreadors* don't kill bulls; that is the *matador's* job — but opera is full of such inconsistencies.) José deserts from his regiment and becomes a smuggler, but Carmen takes up with Escamillo and they meet again outside the bull ring in which he is about to fight. Mad with jealousy, José kills Carmen, who takes the whole thing pretty calmly. After all, it is all a matter of fate, ain't it?

Again, not much of a story but, set to music, what was once a short novel by Prosper Mérimée has become a full-length opera which never fails to draw a huge audience, and deservedly so. *Carmen* is entertainment plus.

Here is a work with everything against it, which works in spite of all. There used to be a standard opening for any summary of *Il trovatore's* plot: 'This is the story of *Il Trovatory*', followed by a synopsis which required a large computer to unravel. Actually, the plot of Verdi's opera is comparatively simple. What goes against it are the conventions of mid-nineteenth century musical works, which are more than offset by the singing, when it is good.

Giuseppe Verdi said: '*Il trovatore* needs only three things: voice, voice and more voice!' He was absolutely correct. This is not an opera, like *Carmen* or *La Bohème* which can be performed successfully with second-rate voices.

Although *Trovatore* came after *Rigoletto* in Verdi's large output of successful operas, it was the last of his early operas — works designed to bring the house down by sheer vocal power and rousing tunes. Plots did not matter. Continuity did not matter. Style did not really matter either. All that was wanted was a fine vehicle for great singers and that is exactly what *Trovatore* is.

The action, and there is a lot of it, all takes place during the intervals. There used to be a lot of intervals, but modern methods of shifting scenery quickly have reduced them to a minimum. Still, there are eight scenes in four acts and in each the characters re-tell what has happened since the curtain fell before the last interval. This was standard practice in those days, but it does not make for clarity, especially when the plots are as complicated as this one is. Obviously, there must be something special about *Il trovatore* to make it such a popular work. There is: the music and the way it is sung.

The key here is neither fate nor curses, but that hoary old chestnut, the mixing up of babies. It would be pointless to list in which interval which thing happens, but in summary the action looks like this: in fifteenth century Spain the mother of the gypsy Azucena was burnt at the stake as a witch by the old Count de Luna. In revenge Azucena took the baby son of the Count and threw him into the flames. Unfortunately, she picked the wrong child and burnt her own son instead. The vision of this haunts

HOW TO

ENJOY

OPERA

WITHOUT

REALLY

TRYING

her still. She has brought up the de Luna boy as her own and he has become an early kind of guerilla leader under the name Manrico. All this happened before the opera begins!

We now find the heroine, Leonora, in love with a mysterious troubadour (Manrico) who serenades under her window each night. The man who officially wants to marry her is the brother of Manrico, the current Count de Luna. Neither, of course, knows the true identity of the other.

Manrico and de Luna are at war, each with an army of his own. Leonora, believing Manrico to have been killed during one of the intervals, chooses to enter a convent. As she is about to do so the Count de Luna comes to kidnap her, only to be met by Manrico with an even bigger band of well-armed men. Exit both armies for another battle.

In the meantime Azucena has been captured and recognised by the Count de Luna. Manrico and Leonora are on the point of being married in their besieged castle when Manrico looks out of the window and sees his mother about to be burnt at the stake. Manrico rushes to the rescue, but he fails and during the next interval he himself is captured. He ends up in prison, while outside Leonora pleads for his life with de Luna. She agrees to marry him (or become his *de facto*) if he will release Manrico. De Luna agrees and Leonora promptly takes a slow-acting poison.

In the dungeons Manrico and Azucena await death, when Leonora comes with news of his release. Unfortunately, Manrico decides to argue with her about the price she has paid until it is too late. Leonora drops dead and de Luna chops off Manrico's head. Only then does Azucena tell him: 'You've just killed your own brother!' We are never told what de Luna does to Azucena after the final curtain falls.

'That was the story of *Il trovatore*'? Nonsense. Not at all. In its proper sequence it all makes perfectly good sense, provided that you can understand what everybody is singing about — or have studied your programme during the intervals. But this is an old-fashioned opera, the kind in which production values are less important. What matters is the music, which is conveniently chopped up into small pieces, and there is not a dud among them from the first moment to the last. No other opera ever written has as many good tunes as this one.

From the ridiculous to the sublime. The most satisfactory of all the blood and thunder operas without a doubt is Puccini's *Tosca*, or *La Tosca* as it is more correctly titled. *Tosca* has a simple, easily understood libretto, well-known arias galore, lots of interesting action and it is the one opera which cannot be updated with high-faluting, modern, nonsensical sets. Its three acts are short and to the point and set in locations which still exist. An abstract *Tosca* would be an absurdity. This is one opera which must be treated like any good historical film or television mini-series, and is.

The original play by Victorien Sardou is followed closely by Puccini, except that all the subsidiary characters have been eliminated. There remain only three central figures in a straight-forward story which, though fiction, is historically authentic. Those who refer to Puccini's 'shabby little shocker' with its torture chamber, fake execution, murder and attempted rape would be technically correct but for the fact this is an opera and not a play. Without the music you would indeed have a little shocker, though it is hard to understand why anyone would call the opera, as opposed to a specific production of it, 'shabby'.

*Tosca* is a music drama in the truest sense of the word and it works beautifully because the glorious arias which adorn it are, as in *Pagliacci*, woven into the fabric of the whole. They are there and easily recognised and world-famous, yet when the painter Cavaradossi sings 'Recondita armonia' in the first act, the aria ends with the sacristan still grumbling about the outsider without spiritual values who ignores the Holy Office, etc. etc. Puccini always made a point of discouraging applause in mid-music and that is as it should be. The flow of dramatic as well as musical action should not be interrupted. (He did not succeed, of course; the public applauds just the same in mid-music.)

The exact date of *Tosca* can be established by references in the text: 17 June 1800. The locations in Rome, the Castel Sant' Angelo, the church of Sant'Andrea della Valle and the interior of the Palazzo Farnese are still there for anyone to see. In these surroundings the singer Floria Tosca and her lover, Mario Cavaradossi, get involved with an underground movement against the occupying Austrians. Scarpia, the Chief of Police,

57

HOW TO

ENJOY

OPERA

WITHOUT

REALLY

TRYING

himself lusts after Tosca. He has Cavaradossi tortured in front of her to find the hiding place of the revolutionary Angelotti. To save Cavaradossi, Tosca reveals the secret. An attempted rape by Scarpia fails, but Tosca promises herself to him if he will spare Cavaradossi and give her a pass for two out of the city. He agrees, writes the pass — and she then kills him.

In the last act Cavaradossi awaits his execution. Tosca arrives to tell him that the execution will be faked; there will be blanks in the guns. But Scarpia's long hand comes from the grave and the blanks turn out to be bullets. Tosca commits suicide.

Short, sharp and to the point and accompanied by glorious music. In the short listings at the end of the book you will find gorier tales than these, but none with music of such immediate appeal. *Tosca* may be a shocker, but what a superb one it is!

# CHAPTER FIVE

# *Spectaculars*

*T*here would seem to be little that the human mind can imagine which has not by now been created visually on film or television by electronic means. You may wonder how modern technology has managed to create special effects which can turn a man into a wolf before your very eyes, which can take you into pitched battle in outer space, or cause motor cars to fly through the air with the greatest of ease. But you do know that it is trickery and deception.

It is difficult to compete with that kind of thing in a theatre, where the illusion has to be actually produced without later editing. We must make a distinction here between technical wizardry and art. The best special effects of stage, films or television have always been those produced by people with creative talents. This is not the place to discuss that abstract thing which is lumped together under the title 'art'; it can take so many forms that nobody will ever agree where art ends and artifice starts.

To make matters worse, there is fashion. What is considered great art today is described as *Kitsch* tomorrow. (*Kitsch* is a German word commonly used to describe something worthless or pretentious or false compared with genuinely inspired work.) It is unfortunately true that art and Kitsch are interchangeable according to the fashion of the day. The old proverb of our ancestors put it much more simply: 'Beauty is in the eye of the

HOW TO

ENJOY

OPERA

WITHOUT

REALLY

TRYING

beholder'. Not only that, but it varies from person to person, though the hypocrite will pretend to like something he hates because it is fashionable to do so. And that is why the word 'arty' has become a derogatory term.

As far as opera is concerned, the contribution of the scenic and costume designer should not be under-estimated. What you see leaves an immediate impression, which can be favourable or unfavourable. Alternatively, if you are an emotional person, it can be exciting or distasteful. The originality of the visual concept and the actions of the singers in the stage picture (the work of the 'producer' or 'director') can make a tremendous difference. The days when singing alone was all that mattered have long gone.

Thus, if your inclinations are toward being impressed by the technical spectacle of a presentation, it is no good starting with a small-scale comedy, no matter how good. There are operas which demand to be mounted with enormous expense and usually are. The use of clever lighting and modern production techniques can bypass the conventional construction of large sets and special effects, and the financial problems of some opera companies can cause even the best to fall back on such short-cuts. Some of the greatest minds of our time have lent their talents to creating sometimes very economical new ideas which have satisfied a lot of people, though it must be admitted that some of the most revolutionary methods have only succeeded over the shortest possible time.

Let me give but one major example of what I mean. The works of Richard Wagner are preserved in a spirit of almost religious fervour in the theatre the composer himself designed and built in Bayreuth. Once a year the faithful from all over the world assemble in Germany under far from ideal conditions to pay tribute at the feet of the long-dead master of the most spectacular kind of opera you could possibly imagine.

God forbid that any newcomer to opera should start at this famous shrine. You will find my reasons for this in Chapter 7, which is truthfully headed 'Boring Operas'. But the happenings at Bayreuth, because of the reverence with which they are treated, will illustrate the point I am trying to make.

Wagner died in 1883 and left most detailed instructions how

*From Russia with Love.* Napoleon enters
Moscow in *War and Peace*. Modern stage craft
can produce battles as good as any in films
these days.
(*War and Peace* by Prokofiev — English
National Opera, London)

HOW TO

ENJOY

OPERA

WITHOUT

REALLY

TRYING

his operas were to be staged. But, while his music has retained its popularity, he was limited in the visual aspects of his productions by the primitive methods at his disposal. Technology has come a long way in the last hundred years! Nobody today would dare to stage a Wagner opera completely faithful to his instructions, but a dragon is a dragon and a giant is a giant and Valhalla is the home of the gods up in heaven. The only things usually omitted after Wagner's death, were the horses. While horses is horses, as has been commonly observed, they also misbehave at the most unexpected times and in the most unexpected places. Exit the horses, but dragons, giants and Valhallas proliferated until Wagner's grandsons, Wieland and Wolfgang, took over the management of Bayreuth after World War II.

Wieland Wagner in particular almost completely abolished all realistic scenery from the Wagner operas, replacing it with lighting effects and symbolic gestures by the singers, who hardly moved at all. The whole world followed suit, not only in Wagner, but in other operas.

But, as time passed, the standing figures of singers on bare stages became boring concerts without dramatic impact and the cycle reversed itself, going to the other extreme. The pioneers came from East Germany, the one operatic country which was communist, yet still had centuries of artistic history behind it. Soon many Wagner operas (in the West as well) became satires on Nazi Germany and that meant productions in modern dress. Wotan, the top god of pre-historic Nordic sagas appeared in a frock-coat and primitive forges making swords became atomic power plants. At present we are halfway back to the realism of the nineteenth century, though we have not reverted to the painted scenery of those days.

What I have said about the Wagner operas applies to a great extent to almost any other opera. Experiments have taken place and a stylised form of realism has taken over. The newcomer to the medium today will usually find something recognisable: people sit on chairs at tables and fight with swords if the action calls for it. And if spectacle is required, we do get it. Thus, should you visit one of the following operas, you will have something to look at if the music does not hold your attention or if the singing is not perhaps as inspiring as you would like it.

It is no coincidence that the majority of pictures in this book are not the kind you may expect. Their purpose is to get you interested in the text, to dip into it and, perhaps, even read a major part of it. Other books are written for *aficionados*, people who love opera and want to see their favourites. (I wish I had a dollar for every picture ever published of Joan Sutherland! Few close-ups of singers do more than satisfy the craving of their fans.) In this book I am trying to show you a world which, partly through the self-indulgence of singers and their fans, has become distorted. There really is more to opera than just singing or being a social butterfly.

What better place for demonstrating one of the many unexpected aspects of opera than in the chapter about 'spectacular' operas? Can you imagine operas being sold out to 25,000 people, as they are during the Verona festival in Italy each year? It must be seen to be believed and on page 68 you will see what it is that draws those crowds to the ancient Roman arena each year. They have good singers, but not the greatest stars — few of those like to risk their million dollar voices in a sudden rain storm. As for the great actor-singers, they don't want to waste their talents on subtle artistry where it can only be appreciated by the spectators with the most expensive field-glasses.

The public has come for the spectacle, for a version of a familiar favourite on the grandest possible scale, a scale vastly greater than any enclosed theatre can duplicate. Yet what I have called 'spectaculars' are the bread-and-butter of every opera house which thinks itself important — and some of the smallest lay claim to that title, some with justification; in 1985 tiny Glyndebourne in the darkest corner of Sussex in southern England staged *Carmen*, an opera which is a staple item at Verona! An opera which can be a spectacle for 800 or 25,000!

Of course, I have chosen the most extreme example. More logically, turn to page 94 and look at the set of Act 2 of *La Bohème* as you can see it today at the Metropolitan Opera House in New York, which built it at a cost of $750,000 in 1982 and can whip it up at will in 15 minutes flat! Only 3,800 people can see that at any one time. Only! But what looks like the whole of the Latin Quarter of Paris is created with modern stage machinery under ideal acoustic conditions where it can, has and will be sung by the

HOW TO

ENJOY

OPERA

WITHOUT

REALLY

TRYING

world's best singers. When they are backed by scenic effects such as these, even the least knowledgeable among my readers will find Puccini's music enhanced to the point where it becomes irresistible.

A handicap, or asset, according to your inclination, is the fact that the desire to hear some beautiful music again and again is accompanied by an overwhelming desire for the unusual, even sensational, in the staging of familiar works. For the newcomer to opera any well-staged performance of a popular but, to him or her, as yet unknown, opera will give great pleasure. But opera is addictive and once you get it in large doses year after year, your favourite works of the moment can become wearisome on the visual side. The point is reached when a recorded or videotaped performance will do just as well. Since the regular opera-goer is the backbone of every subscription series, even traditional opera houses have been experimenting with sometimes revolutionary (and occasionally revolting) alternatives to what our fathers and grandfathers took for granted.

I remember a well-known critic, who in all seriousness condemned an excellent production of *La Bohème* solely on the grounds that its Mimì entered from the side instead of the back of the artists' attic, as laid down by Puccini. That critic was a traditionalist whose prejudices looked backwards. The new extremists among opera producers are those who go way beyond such simple liberties with instructions set down by the composer who, at the time of the first production, also acted as producer/director. (Many things were different in those days!) In recent years we have had some outrageous visual distortions of standard works, while their music remained note perfect and uncut. Many were imitated so often that they in turn became as tiresome as the traditional methods. For example, in the 1960s it became almost compulsory to find Nazi stormtroopers and the swastika in any major Wagner revival.

Not only scenery, but costumes and production (the actions designed for the principals and chorus) have long ago exceeded the limits which would have been set by even the most imaginative composer even though the music remains the same after a century or even two. Rather than describe particularly outrageous instances of modern opera productions — some of which exceed anything ever invented for any video-clip — let me offer you a few descriptive quotes which appeared in an opera magazine chosen at random. Believe me, the following are not carefully chosen items to prove a possibly non-existent point, but the result of a quick glance through a monthly publication, London's *Opera* of June 1985:

'A posse of body-snatchers ... whose final offering was the accusing, beheaded corpse of Marguerite.'
*Faust* (Vienna State Opera)

'... making you feel physically ill-at-ease ... Having seen the work in London I took the precaution of not eating beforehand.'
*The Devils of Loudun* (Penderecki) (Strasbourg, France)

'*Pagliacci* — wait for it — in a contemporary tenement-block ... Tonio arrived on stage driving a motor-bike.'
Basle, Switzerland

'A poster of Mrs Thatcher had dollar signs replacing her eyes ... the god ... was President Reagan in a tutu ...'
*Mahagonny Singspiel* (Weill) (Queen Elizabeth Hall, London)

'Seemed to take place in a huge public lavatory ... with walls on which vacuous graffiti were painted during the performance.'
*Don Giovanni* (Scottish Opera)

Not all the above were necessarily concerned with bad productions or operas of which the writer disapproved. There is room for the new as well as the old. I might as well quote the opposite view from the same issue of the same magazine.

'After more than a quarter-of-a-century much of the production still looks well and the magic ... still works.'
*Don Carlos* (Covent Garden, London)

My point is that today's opera revival can partly be laid at the feet of those who have turned their backs on the old fashioned, expected kind of production. There is a trend back toward the traditional which, in the light of excesses, such as some of those quoted above, is understandable. But never again will we see bland, painted castles and static singers mouthing their words.

La donna *is* mobile *all right! Rigoletto* and other operas have been adapted to suit many periods. Sixteenth century Italian seductions and murder have been enacted in other periods with equal success. Rigoletto as a Mafia hit-man in New York and as an official in Mussolini's Italy.
(*Above: Rigoletto* by Verdi — English National Opera, London)
(*Below: Rigoletto* by Verdi — Victoria State Opera, Melbourne)

Going to the opera can be an exciting experience, whether the production 'still has magic after twenty-five years' or whether some completely new outrageous idea has produced a box-office success.

If you need any other comparisons with things other than the video-clips with which I have equated pop opera a little too often perhaps, remember the most famous musicals of recent years, from *Hair* to *Cats* and you will find that they invariably have been associated with productions which break all the rules. For every success in their field there were a dozen failures, and you can say the same about opera, except that here there is a known factor: the unchanging, and usually familiar, music. If, as I have suggested, shows like *Cats* become operettas and ultimately operas, they will not be replicas of the original. In fact, *Cats* is already being staged all over the world, each new production being totally different from the last. Why is it so? Perhaps *Cats* will survive on the music. Perhaps it is an opera already!

## AIDA

The most spectacular effects in today's opera houses are not to be found in the best-selling operas. It is the less famous works which need the awe-inspiring sets: a real Trojan Horse, big enough to hold a hundred men, in Berlioz' *The Trojans*; or a genuine parting of the Red Sea for Rossini's *Moses in Egypt*. But there are some popular works for which, to succeed at the box office, any major company must turn on the spectacle.

Strangely, the most famous of these is, strictly speaking, an intimate opera with but one necessarily grand scene, Verdi's *Aida*. The 'Triumphal March' from this is one of the best-known tunes in the world and many of its arias are familiar indeed. In these days of modern multi-purpose sets (sets which can be used in whole or in part in more than one scene) the need for the Victory March of the Egyptians after having conquered Ethiopia inevitably tempts the designer to extend his gigantic sets into the other acts as well. There are two temples and an exterior by the River Nile; and, for good measure, why not enact the entombment of the lovers at the end in a pyramid-like structure?

*'Rain stops play'*, not only at cricket or tennis,
but in the open-air Arena of Verona, Italy, where
25,000 people watch opera at each
performance.
(*Aida* by Verdi — Arena di Verona)

A six-foot hole in the ground would do just as well — but audiences expect something bigger than that!

I think you can confidently go and see *Aida* and be dazzled by its splendour; no company will stage it and disappoint its audience. However, it is the personal fate of its characters which makes *Aida* the popular success which it is, not the scenery.

The action is set during the rule of the Pharaohs, long before Cleopatra. The King of Egypt is making war on Ethiopia and appoints Radamès to lead the army. His daughter Amneris and her slave Aida both love Radamès, but he has eyes only for Aida. The battle is won and the army returns in triumph, carrying immense amounts of booty and hundreds of prisoners. The King offers the victor Amneris as his wife.

But among the prisoners is Amonasro, Aida's father, who is also the King of Ethiopia. Radamès accidentally gives away the plans of the army he commands to Aida and is overheard by Amonasro. Brought to trial for treason before the priests, Radamès refuses to recant in spite of Amneris' pleas and he is condemned to be buried alive. In the tomb he finds that Aida has joined him voluntarily and they die together.

*Aida* abounds with famous tunes. One of the world's great tenor arias 'Celeste Aida' begins the opera and one of its most glorious duets ends it. The 'Triumphal March' with its celebrated ensemble of trumpets and massed choruses, through which both tenor and soprano have to cut with tremendous top notes, is one of the glories in all of opera. Not to be missed.


## TURANDOT

The last opera by the most popular composer of operas, Giacomo Puccini, was incomplete at his death in 1924; the final duet had been sketched, but not completed. The job was done by someone else, but *Turandot* was not the instant hit everybody expected. It is not easy to understand what held up its general acceptance, when it contained music such as the ever-popular tenor aria 'Nessun dorma' ('None shall sleep'). But the title rôle is one of the most difficult to cast convincingly and the really great Turandots of past and present can be counted on the fingers of one hand.

HOW TO

ENJOY

OPERA

WITHOUT

REALLY

TRYING

Nevertheless, the flow of melody did not desert Puccini. Though Turandot is a very difficult part for any soprano to sing, he wrote the loveliest music for the second lead, Liù, a typical Puccini heroine in the mould of Mimì and Butterfly. The tenor is handsomely served and the spectacle is second only to *Aida*.

The subject is again exotic, this time ancient China. The beautiful Princess Turandot refuses to marry any man who cannot answer three riddles she sets. Failure to do so means death to the suitor. Yet they come in droves, besotted by the double prize of a lovely woman and the throne of China. The man known as 'The Unknown Prince' arrives with his father Timur and the slave girl Liù. He does answer Turandot's riddles correctly, but she cannot bear to be beaten. Then the Prince makes an offer: if Turandot can guess his name, he will not claim his prize — hence she gives the order: 'None shall sleep' until his name is found. Turandot has Liù tortured to extract the Prince's name, but the girl commits suicide rather than betray him.

At this point Puccini died, but Franco Alfano completed the final-duet in which Calaf reveals his name to Turandot, but she now in turn refuses to accept the easy way out. Presumably they live happily ever after, each having lost his/her head for love.

*Turandot* may be a static opera and not everybody at first takes to the strange courtiers Ping, Pang and Pong (I do not joke, those are their names) who interrupt the flow of the action, yet can be very melodious and amusing when well-acted and well-sung. But few companies can resist the opportunity for scenic splendour which ancient China offers and the music is never less than tuneful.

My last two examples of 'spectacular' operas may be slightly misleading, for both can be produced on the cheap without the necessary spectacle and have been so produced. However, the operas listed in detail in each chapter are supposed to be suitable for immediate consumption by the casual visitor and the two other types of spectacular operas, 'grand operas' and 'magical operas', are not generally accepted 'pop operas' for reasons which I shall explain.

I have chosen *Faust* as an example of what is known as 'grand opera'. People quite wrongly speak of 'grand' operas as opposed

to ordinary operas. The fact is that until well into the twentieth
century the term 'grand' really meant what it said. Its prophet
was Giacomo Meyerbeer, whose operas were vastly more popular than those of any other composer for the best part of a
century. His *Les Huguenots* was presented world-wide and always
billed as 'The Night of the Seven Stars' because it had seven principals and every theatre used its best singers in each of the seven
rôles.

Grand operas were the works to which I referred in Chapter 1,
the ones which always featured volcanoes, floods, fires, shipwrecks, avalanches and the like, the ones in which the latest
scenic effects were as important as the singers. As in the case of
Wagner, those scenic effects today would look pretty ridiculous
compared with what we have seen in our own homes on television or in cinemas. The music of Meyerbeer and his kind is not
in the Wagner class, but it is quite easy to stage Gounod operas
like *Faust* or *Romeo and Juliet* as grand operas, for they provide
opportunities for all the necessary spectacle, provided that
the company presenting them is willing to be historically
accurate.

The story of *Faust* is that of a literary masterpiece by the
German Johann Wolfgang von Goethe, but the Gounod version
concerns itself with only a small part of it. (An Italian, Arrigo
Boito, made a better stab at the deeper meaning of Goethe's
play, but his *Mefistofele* can hardly be classed as a pop opera, as
*Faust* can.) Like all French grand operas, *Faust* is extremely long;
it has five acts and includes a long, and very popular, ballet as
well. *Faust* is usually shortened in some way, but its endless
stream of familiar melodies and many scenes make only the
usual cutting of the ballet a cause for complaint.

## FAUST

Faust is a medieval German philosopher who seeks to regain his
lost youth by selling his soul to the devil, Mephistopheles, who
swings the old man his way by showing him a vision of a young
girl, Marguerite. The rejuvenated Faust meets Marguerite at a
village fair and in due course seduces her. She bears a child, goes

HOW TO

ENJOY

OPERA

WITHOUT

REALLY

TRYING

mad and is imprisoned. Mephisto and an Angelic Host fight for Marguerite's soul as she dies in jail and she goes up, of course, not down, much to Mephisto's chagrin. He has to be satisfied with Faust alone.

The famous ballet takes place on Walpurgis Night where Faust meets all the great beauties of history.

It does not seem much of a story for spectacle, but a lot can be made of the Village Fair (again with ballet), the soldiers going off to war, singing one of the most famous opera choruses ever written, not to mention Valentine's aria 'Even bravest heart may swell', the elaborate Garden Scene with its wonderful Love Duet, the macabre Church Scene in which Marguerite is tempted by Mephisto and, of course, her ascent to Heaven from the prison.

*Faust* was for many years the most popular opera in the repertoire. The Metropolitan Opera House in New York was at one time referred to as the *Faustspielhaus*, which translates as: the house which plays *Faust*, a pun on Wagner's Bayreuth *Festspielhaus* (Festival Playhouse).


THE MAGIC FLUTE

Inclusion of *The Magic Flute* among spectacular operas may come as an even greater surprise, but this is the one Mozart work which should be staged spectacularly, but rarely is. It is in reality a nonsensical pantomime invented by the actor Emanuel Schikaneder as a vehicle for his own talents. (He created the rôle of Papageno for himself.) The choice of Mozart to write the music was coincidental, but the score he produced contains so many famous arias, duets and ensembles that it has immortalised an otherwise complete nonentity, Schikaneder.

*The Magic Flute* is not a grand opera, it belongs to a type known as '*Zauberoper*' (magic opera), existing mainly as an excuse to present supernatural happenings. There are quite a few of these still around, but none are in the *Magic Flute* class, hence its inclusion here. *Zauberopern* give ample scope for spectacular effects and when presented in a theatre like the Salzburg Festival Theatre, they can be as grand as any spectacle you can see anywhere. Unfortunately, the popularity of the work is so great that it is staged far too frequently by companies which are quite unable to produce the required special effects and care should be taken in investigating the production before starting a novice with this work. Apart from the endless stream of familiar melodies, it can make a pretty confusing evening.

Among the 'magic' effects open to the producer's and designer's inventiveness are a giant snake or dragon, people having to pass tests of walking through fire and water, flying genii, Egyptian temples, subterranean caverns, a magic flute which conjures up strange animals, a set of magic bells which turns rapists into rap-dancers and much more.

The Christmas pantomimes of this century and the *Zauberopern* have one thing in common. They were meant to amuse, amaze and entertain children as well as adults. The demise of the modern pantomime was largely due to the fact that theatre audiences today (children included) are too sophisticated to accept the inconsistencies of so many plots. This did not apply in Mozart's time and, ultimately, it is Mozart's music and not his backer, Schikaneder's, illogical plot which has caused *The Magic Flute* to survive.

The main hero and heroine of *The Magic Flute* are Tamino and Pamina, who have to pass a series of tests to raise them to some unexplained higher level in the future of their magical world. Musicologists and historians hopelessly confuse the issue because Mozart and Schikaneder were masons and used some masonic symbols in their opera-cum-pantomime, which is set in ancient Egypt, centuries before freemasonry was invented. Students of freemasonry can have fun picking out the various allusions to their secret rites. They neither add nor detract from what is an enjoyable, if confusing major part of the operatic repertoire.

Pamina is the daughter of the Queen of the Night, who claims that the villainous priest Sarastro has abducted her. Confusion reigns in this part of the story, because at the halfway mark in the opera it suddenly turns out that the kindly Sarastro is only protecting Pamina against the villainous Queen of the Night. Nobody knows why Schikaneder changed sides in mid-stream, but Mozart's flow of melody is not interrrupted.

Mention must also be made of Papageno, the bird-catcher to

HOW TO

ENJOY

OPERA

WITHOUT

REALLY

TRYING

the Queen. He is the most amusing central comedy lead, who wants no more than to find a wife as funny or crazy as he is. Schikaneder wrote this part for himself to play and gives it undue prominence in the action, while Mozart wrote some of his most inspired music for him. Against his will Papageno gets involved in Tamino's quest and their various adventures keep the action moving fast and furious. It would be pointless to list all the characters who appear briefly. Their motives or very existence are vague and inconclusive. Arguments about the meaning, if any, of *The Magic Flute* have raged for nearly two hundred years and this is hardly the place to join into the fray.

To sum up, *The Magic Flute* is a musical delight from end to end and can be a delicious spectacle. All it lacks is rhyme or reason. And let all those who say that that can be said about all opera beware. It simply isn't so! Except in the case of *The Magic Flute*, of course.

# CHAPTER SIX

# Romantic Operas

*T*he word most frequently to be found set to music is un-doubtedly 'love'. Since not too many words rhyme with love, song-writers and librettists have explored just about every sub-stitute or synonym which exists, but it all comes back to the same thing, which one song at least summarises very neatly: 'Love makes the world go round'.

I have no idea how many novels have been written since the printing press was invented, but there would be very few which do not have some kind of a love story in them. And, since opera is an extension of drama and historical happenings in music form, opera also has its share of love stories. As for my 'historical happenings', you would be surprised how many very major events in history were tied to love affairs or loveless marriages and the like. Unfortunately operas and novels, like Shakespeare's plays, rarely bear any resemblance to the reality of history and we must not accept the romantic entanglements of famous people as they are portrayed in operas as factual. Very few are, more's the pity. Yet the fact is that false history continues to have an immense following world-wide because it has been set to music.

If you have ever been in love, or if that pleasure is still ahead of you, you must know that it lifts you on to a higher emotional plane. In the words of another song: 'I hear music and there's no

*Love all-embracing — literally!* Wagner's two extremes: 'Here comes the bride' from *Lohengrin*, accepted at any church wedding, came from the same pen which has Siegmund and Sieglinde — brother and sister — begatting Siegfried.
(*Lohengrin* by Wagner — Bayrische Staatsoper, Munich)
(*Die Walküre* by Wagner — Australian Opera)

one there'. People in love sing to each other and if they can't sing in tune, it makes no difference at all. Under the circumstances, love and passion are the most obvious subjects for musical treatment and opera and its lighter cousins usually reach their peak of perfection in love duets or their opposite, violent scenes brought about, usually through misunderstandings, by that monstrous side-effect of love: jealousy.

The so-called 'romantic' movement of the nineteenth century added a further dimension to opera, ordinary fiction and even real life. The culmination of a great love in death was fashionable for the greater part of a century. Ideally, people died through sheer ecstasy — they had reached the most glorious fulfilment of life. Why spoil it by going back to the prosaic daily grind? If the 'romantics' had had their way, the human race would not have lasted long!

The ideal was Wagner's *Liebestod* (Love Death — dying of love without the help of poison, dagger or any outside assistance) as suffered by Isolde in *Tristan and Isolde*. But dying of a mental process does stretch credulity. We hear a lot about people dying of 'a broken heart'. The nineteenth century's ideal was the very opposite: people died out of sheer happiness because they were joined with their loved one. Still, the method had its limitations and, as long as love and death went together, composers had many other options. Suicide pacts, death to save a loved one's honour, usually in a most unnecessary duel, or choosing death in preference to what used to be called a 'fate worse than death', that is: giving in to a man other than the one you love. The fact that it should today be necessary to explain that phrase, which in my own youth was commonplace, explains something of why the romantic movement has died a natural death — everywhere but in opera.

Love and death are the lifeblood of opera. And, as Shakespeare's *Romeo and Juliet* refuses to disappear into the mists of history, so do romantic operas draw the crowds year after year. In one case it is the music of the words written by the world's greatest playwright, in the other it is the music of major composers. The present vogue for opera in the original language, because it enhances the flow of the music, proves that operas, such as those I am about to list, survive on the strength and

HOW TO

ENJOY

OPERA

WITHOUT

REALLY

TRYING

quality of the singing, though here also there are examples of works which have a following even when sung by inferior artists. It should be noted that the most successful of these are the ones which have sweeping tunes from the orchestra pit to make up for any shortcomings on stage.

To provide almost ludicrous proof with one example only: in *Madam Butterfly* the unfortunate heroine sings a short phrase ending with: 'He has come back and he loves me!', ordinary stuff in any love story and musically nothing very spectacular for the singer portraying Butterfly. But Puccini follows those words with an *orchestral* climax of such power that audiences regularly interrupt it with a storm of applause, much to the gratification of the soprano, who really had nothing whatever to do with it.

## LA BOHÈME

I think the most fool-proof romantic opera with which to introduce any newcomer to the new medium is Puccini's *La Bohème* and it is very simple to explain in some detail why this is so.

For a start, let me remind you that opera is drama with music and not music with drama. The subject of *La Bohème* is based on a French play which was in turn based on a series of stories which appeared in a Paris magazine in the 1840s. You could say that the series was a pre-television equivalent of today's soap operas which hold their audience week after week until the characters become real people to their audience.

The stories inspired two famous composers to turn them into opera and, in fact, two *Bohèmes* exist, one by Puccini and the other by Leoncavallo, the composer of *Pagliacci*. Puccini's was not the instant hit people may think and even today Leoncavallo has advocates who think his contains better music. Never mind, Puccini won the race and it is Puccini's *Bohème* with which I deal. Still, it is worth remembering that the story was good enough to inspire a feud between two old friends, which resulted in two individual works — each composer knew the other was at work on the same subject! It really was some soap opera! And it still is; witness the avalanche of handkerchiefs to be seen as the final curtain falls.

*A love which has* no *name*. The hero marries an
orange! The one on the right.
(*The Love of Three Oranges* by Prokofiev —
Sadler's Wells Opera, London)

HOW TO

ENJOY

OPERA

WITHOUT

REALLY

TRYING

Starting with a first-class story, it only needed truly popular music to produce a masterpiece which can please an audience, even with an inferior cast. I have seen some stinkers in my time, but none ever concluded with anything but reasonable applause from the audience. Puccini belonged to the *verismo* school (see Chapter 4) and wrote continuous music with no gaps during which audiences could applaud arias. Yet the end of *La Bohème's* first act alone has two straight arias and a love duet, one and all meant to be heard in silence. They are famous enough to be mentioned here: 'Your tiny hand is frozen', 'They call me Mimì' and 'Lovely maid in the moonlight'. And that is only the start! The rest of the opera never falls far below that standard and contains other highlights equally well-known. Consider that in addition the action never flags and you begin to understand why this opera is performed somewhere or other in the world every day every year.

*La Bohème* is, of course, a love story. In fact, it is two love stories. (Remember, it is a non-television soap opera.) There are two pairs of lovers, Mimì and Rodolfo, a poet, and Musetta and Marcello, the painter who shares a room with him. They live in the artists' quarter of Paris and are so poor that both girls have to sell their bodies at some stage of the story or perish.

Mimì and Rodolfo meet in his garret in the first act. In the second they join their friends for supper in the Café Momus. There we meet Musetta, the ex-lover of Marcello, at present attached to a rich admirer, who has, by coincidence, brought her to the same café. Musetta is bright, flighty and much prefers her Marcello, who is the jealous type. The admirer is dumped, and both couples, followed by half of Paris, march off in triumph.

Time passes before the third act begins. Mimì has tuberculosis and is getting weaker every day. Musetta and Marcello are fighting like cat and dog. Rodolfo (sensitive soul) cannot bear to see Mimì suffer, but cannot help her. Marcello must watch Musetta making money on the side, ostensibly by giving singing lessons. Both couples decide to part.

In the last act the two men are back in the garret, alone, when Musetta brings the dying Mimì to see Rodolfo. Mimì dies, of course, but we are left to assume that her death has brought the other couple together again.

The final seal of approval for Puccini's *Bohème* lies in the fact that it gives immense scope for imaginative, and even spectacular sets. See illustration on page 94. It is a designer's dream and a good producer cannot fail with this work. I defy anyone to be bored by a viewing of this opera.

## LA TRAVIATA

In choosing 'romantic' operas for beginners, Puccini's *Bohème* was the odd man out, for it is the only popular opera which has much else to recommend it apart from the familiar music and the handkerchiefs which are an essential part of the audience's equipment. The others suffer a handicap which may well steer away some newcomers to opera. Both are tragic love stories with music which is most appealing. Yet both lack action. Visiting Verdi's *La traviata* involves long stretches of watching singers making beautiful music without anything happening, though there are two exceptional scenes, one of beauty and the other of action.

The word *traviata* is not a name, but a description. Many years ago people translated it as 'the frail one'. Well, Violetta Valery, like Mimì, is a victim of the dreaded consumption and she also dies of it in the end. Yet her life and story are at the opposite end of the social spectrum. Violetta is a high-priced callgirl, one of whose clients, Alfredo Germont, falls in love with her at a brilliant ball in her Paris home. (Actually Violetta and Alfredo were real people whose troubles were autobiographical and made the original Alfredo, Alexandre Dumas, jun., world famous. *The Lady of the Camellias* is better known as *Camille* since Garbo starred in the film of the play.)

Act 2 finds Alfredo installed in Violetta's country home, she having given up her life of shame (nineteenth-century style). Unknown to him she has been selling off her jewels and other things to keep up their life-style. Then she is visited by Alfredo's father, usually referred to simply as Germont. Treating Violetta as a courtesan at first, he soon realises that this is a noble woman who truly loves his son. Unfortunately, her past would seriously interfere with Alfredo's life and that of his family. He asks her to

81

HOW TO

ENJOY

OPERA

WITHOUT

REALLY

TRYING

give him up — and she does. It is a very long and very beautiful scene musically, but decidedly static.

To break the relationship Violetta returns to her old life and in a dramatic confrontation in a gambling salon Alfredo insults her publicly, only to be reprimanded, equally publicly, by his father, who arrives at the crucial moment.

In the last act Violetta is mortally ill. Germont has relented and told his son the truth. Alfredo arrives for a last minute reconciliation, but it is too late by then. Violetta dics rather beautifully. Actually, the whole opera is rather beautiful, especially for sentimentalists or music-lovers. Long stretches of the music are world-famous and only those seeking visual distraction may become restless through one or two lengthy duets. But that is a failing with romantic subjects in any field; James Bond fans are unlikely to buy Barbara Cartland novels, aren't they?

## MADAM BUTTERFLY

I have to include *Madam Butterfly* among my romantic operas, though it does give Puccini two out of three. But then, Puccini was a womaniser and it was the suffering heroines of his operas who made his name immortal. Even in the highly dramatic *Turandot*, the minor character of the slave girl Liù is the most human and has the loveliest music.

There is no doubt that *Madam Butterfly* contains some of Puccini's most accessible melodies and that practically everybody knows them. To start with the one and only handicap which besets this most famous of romantic operas: if you removed all the repeats of those famous tunes, the opera would be half the length it is.

There is something in opera known as *Leitmotive*, meaning literally 'leading motives' or, more accurately, signature tunes. Wagner supposedly invented these, because he carries their use to illogical extremes. Others before Wagner had used the idea first, but he claimed the credit and most still believe that this is so. Theoretically, you could listen to a Wagner opera and, if you know the various tunes which go with various characters or actions, you could understand the whole thing, even without the words.

Puccini in *Madam Butterfly* has no great selection of *Leitmotive*, but he does have one or two immediately recognisable tunes which he trots out again and again. Happily, they are the kind of things which Mum and Dad and the kids can hum, whistle or even sing without too much trouble. Consequently the music of *Butterfly* becomes familiar very quickly and it is so tuneful that only odd curmudgeons like me who, you must remember, have heard the opera umpteen times grumble into their beards, if any: 'What? Not again!' That, of course cannot apply to the newcomer, who will welcome tunes which have not become hackneyed — for they are good tunes — with open arms.

The story-line of *Madam Butterfly* can be told in a very few words: in Nagasaki Lieutenant Pinkerton of the U.S. Navy in about 1910 'marries' a Japanese teenager under Japanese law which, to him, means nothing at all. The marriage has been arranged by a marriage broker. The entrance of the bride to the elaborate traditional Japanese wedding which follows is a musical gem, but the latter is interrupted violently by the Bonze (a Japanese priest), who curses Butterfly for renouncing her old faith for Pinkerton. The love duet which ends the first act is quite possibly the most famous in all of opera.

Three years later Butterfly has borne Pinkerton a child and is still patiently waiting for his return. The American consul, Sharpless, brings a letter in English to Butterfly to say that Pinkerton has now married an American, but his ship (and wife) will return to Nagasaki shortly. Butterfly simply cannot understand Sharpless, who is over-subtle in trying to spare her feelings; all she knows is that her husband is about to return. When Pinkerton's ship actually enters the harbour, she and her faithful servant Suzuki joyously decorate their house and sit up all night so that they may be ready to greet him as soon as he arrives. And so he does the following day, only to find that he has a son of whom he knew nothing.

The truth dawns on Butterfly only when she first sees the new Mrs Pinkerton and she commits hara-kiri, the traditional form of Japanese suicide. The oriental setting, while intimate, makes for a great difference in looks compared with other operas and the various minor characters lend plenty of colour to the proceedings. The music, even in its most dramatic moments, is eminently

HOW TO

ENJOY

OPERA

WITHOUT

REALLY

TRYING

tuneful and even the slow interludes, such as the 'Humming Chorus' which denotes the passing of night is sheer magic. *Madam Butterfly* will live as long as opera and is immediately acceptable by anyone without prejudice for other types of opera or music.

# CHAPTER SEVEN

# Boring Operas

*I*t may seem extraordinary to include a chapter with a heading such as this, but it is an essential ingredient in making sure that the reader will not get the wrong idea of what this, to him, strange medium is all about. Chances are that in childhood, or later, he or she will have been told that opera is an esoteric art which is only for those who 'understand' it (whatever that may mean) or for snobs who want to become society butterflies, or perhaps for those lunatics who are fascinated with opera, as others are fascinated with the love life of spiders or similar strange subjects.

I have said before that the term 'opera' covers an immense variety of subjects and types of music. I cannot believe that any one person would like every opera there is, though the genuine opera-lover may well experiment by going to see things which they ultimately find dull. This chapter is not devoted to the operas which are boring because they are bad operas or unsuitable for anyone with an inquisitive mind; quite the contrary.

Some of the greatest masterpieces of the operatic art are likely to bore the average person unless or until he or she has seen a fair amount of opera and is thoroughly familiar with it. What would a teenager feel or do if asked to eat a raw oyster? Ask yourself that and then put the same question to someone who has become a gourmet after having explored the best restaurants in the world.

HOW TO

ENJOY

OPERA

WITHOUT

REALLY

TRYING

The latter may never have tried a raw oyster for whatever reason, but would know that it is considered a delicacy. Why not try one? He or she might become an immediate addict or dislike the experience. But it would be a decision taken on the basis of a thorough knowledge of what people eat and drink and if the verdict is negative, so what? There is a lot of other food which can be enjoyed and let those who want to, have their oysters and eat them as well! The teenager's reaction is likely to be less predictable.

Translate all that nonsense into opera, or any other kind of music and it becomes obvious that some people like romantic operas, others like modern music and a minority prefer the primitive tones of renaissance tunes, preferably played on ancient instruments. Some might enjoy the first and the second or any other combination of the three. Few would like all of them equally. Rather than be specific about individual works, as in earlier chapters, let me offer you generalisations about various kinds of music which are likely to be boring *if you start your opera-going in these particular fields.*

In the Quick Check List at the end of the main text you can assess individual works. For the moment let us concentrate on some generalities.

## BAROQUE OPERAS

Music drama in the operatic sense did not start properly until the late eighteenth century and operas by masters as famous as Handel can fail to enchant even regular opera-goers. The rare producer who in the 1980s has applied modern production techniques to the works of Handel or Rameau or Vivaldi has sometimes met the approval of regular opera audiences. I doubt whether the novice would not be bored by them. Regardless of production gimmicks, they are exercises in vocal acrobatics, consisting almost exclusively of solo arias. As for 'authentic' productions from pre-Mozart days: stay away, unless the baroque is your cup of tea anyway.

The reality of the matter is that music and opera started out as the plaything of the aristocracy, if not royalty itself. Louis XIV was one of the founders of classical ballet, for example, and a dancer himself. Thus music written in the seventeenth and early eighteenth centuries was not intended for the likes of you and me, but for a specialised public which had conventions which are long dead. One of the most obvious differences in the field of opera was the *castrato*, a man who had been castrated in child-hood to preserve the beauty of his childish soprano voice. We have no *castrati* today and don't really know what they sounded like. But they were the great and highly paid opera stars of their time. Everything they did and everything that anybody else did on an opera stage was different from what is normally done today. Unless there is a genuine interest in the period on the part of the newcomer to opera, it is unlikely that any modern attempt to re-stage what went on in Handel's time and before will be enjoyable, or give the novice any idea what opera is all about. Probably he or she will be bored stiff.

## WAGNER

Although the heading of this part is the name of a single composer, his is the one name which is constantly in the public eye and in public demand. This is not the place to discuss Wagner, the man, or the music of Wagner in detail. Suffice to say that more has been written about both than about any other composer. And, strangely enough, there are many pages of Wagner which you, the newcomer, would find very tuneful in-deed; I am sure you know some or all of the following: The 'Wedding March' from *Lohengrin*, the 'Entry of the Guests' and 'O Star of Eve' from *Tannhäuser*, the 'Prize Song' from *The Mastersingers of Nuremberg*, the 'Ride of the Valkyries' from *Die Walküre* and all those glorious overtures. You may even have heard and loved 'Brünnhilde's Immolation' from *Die Götterdämmerung!* If only it were possible to assemble the great popular moments from all the Wagner operas in one evening, linked by an appropriate story, of course. Alas, it is not possible, and I very much regret that the whole of his works are, I feel, out of bounds as introductions to opera for newcomers to the art.

Wagner may have been a most important figure in the history

HOW TO

ENJOY

OPERA

WITHOUT

REALLY

TRYING

of opera. In his own time he himself authorised and even conducted heavily cut versions of his own works to make them easier for audiences to whom he was not known at all. Today the fashion is to play everything uncut. That means that even the most accessible Wagner, *Lohengrin* and *Tannhäuser*, involve four hours in a theatre, far too much for anyone not already familiar with the art form.

Only recently I was approached by an elderly gentleman who confided to me that at the age of seven he was taken to see *Tristan and Isolde*, a work containing hours of beautiful, but continuous, music. He did not return to the opera house until he was in his forties! Now, in his declining years he even attends lectures on opera by John Cargher! There must be a moral in there somewhere, if only I can explain it in some way.

Someone once wrote (I think it was George Bernard Shaw) that 'Wagner is oases of beauty and deserts of boredom'. And Sir Thomas Beecham, who conducted Wagner superbly, said: 'Isn't Wagner an old bore!' The admirer of 'Brünnhilde's Immolation' might remember that the whole of *Die Götterdämmerung* occupies, depending on the conductor, a little more or a little less than six hours! (It is usually performed with a long dinner interval, which must be added to the time taken by the music!)

It is quite possible, even likely, that Wagner made his operas so long because in his time the public expected four- to six- hour performances, which usually consisted of an opera, a ballet, a play and various variety acts in between. By making his operas quite so long, the performance of anything else on the same night became an impossibility.

More important, Wagner revolutionised conventional opera and did away with what I might loosely term tunes, that is, arias and set pieces calling for individual applause. His earlier works, *Rienzi, Lohengrin* or *Tannhäuser* still retained a few of the said 'tunes', but thereafter his ideas of creating complete fusion between word, music and stage spectacle took over and the approach to opera via Wagner of any kind is extremely dangerous. While *Lohengrin* might prove bearable (only four hours!) a first visitor to opera faced with *Parsifal* would probably not last the performance, let alone come back for more.

88

No, leave Wagner for later. *The Ring of the Nibelungen* is an acknowledged masterpiece in this field, but not for beginners. Let us walk before starting on that kind of marathon.

## MODERN OPERAS

Unless, for reasons which could be many, you have been brought up with modern music as your regular diet, keep away from it. Of course, there are exceptions, as there are with Wagner, but in general terms anything written after 1925 should be avoided, unless it is a musical of some sort, of course.

At the beginning of this century a gentleman named Arnold Schoenberg revolted against the conventional kind of music, the harmonic structure of which was used by all the great composers of the past, including Wagner. The influence of Schoenberg and his followers was immense, but produced a very limited number of operas which are universally accepted. Even a standard repertory work like Alban Berg's *Wozzeck* (1925) is likely to put experienced opera-lovers to flight; I have seen them leave in mid-act at some of the best performances I have attended.

In more recent years the ideas of Schoenberg have been superseded by an 'anything goes' attitude. The only virtue a newcomer could find in the operas of today is the immense advances which have been made in staging techniques and you may well find an opera which entertains you visually by its brilliant scenery and bizarre production. But don't think that this is a representation of what is universally known as 'opera'. It may well be staged at a world-famous opera house, say, La Scala or the Metropolitan, but if you are interested in eventually becoming an addict Sam Goldwyn's advice would have been: 'Include me out.'

On the other hand, it would be unfair not to mention what some people prefer to call 'music theatre' rather than opera. In very general terms, this is a highly original subject which is accompanied by very modern music, unlikely to appeal to a newcomer on its own merits, but highly suitable as — dare I say it? — background music to a good play.

It will be found that the only modern operas which get revived with reasonable regularity are works with brilliant libretti or

*Trying to make a monkey out of you?* No, Hans
Werner Henze in *The Young Lord* tries to make
a man out of a monkey. There is little music, but
a fascinating story and spectacle.
(*Der junge Lord* by Henze — Staatsoper,
Vienna)

fascinating subjects. A lot of people want to see these and it takes a while before that demand is fulfilled; few new operas are performed more than three or four times initially.

Take the case of Hans Werner Henze's *Der junge Lord* (The Young Lord), a morality play about a man who introduces a monkey into café society in a small town as a foreign aristocrat wishing to settle down and marry. The efforts of the citizens to entertain the stranger can be very funny in a good production. But how many times would you want to see *Der junge Lord?*

Lovers of the macabre may be interested in *The Devils of Loudun* by Penderecki, which deals with a seventeenth-century witch trial and graphically shows (on stage!) the literal breaking of a man's legs and arms, nuns in orgiastic ecstasy and, depending on the producer, a fair amount of nudity. If you can whistle even two bars of Penderecki's music, you are a better man than I am!

The in-between works can hold attractions which, while they are not fair introductions to opera, can strike a happy medium — an accidental pun, for Menotti's *The Medium* is probably the most successful of them all. This is first class theatre by any standard. Like most Menotti works it turns up with an occasional good tune and the mystery story (which I will not reveal) is as gripping as anything you can see on television.

These are not 'boring' works, but works which should not be taken as typical. They stand individually, seeking repeat business only from those who have acquired the taste for this or that composer's particular musical oyster. They are best left alone, unless you have prior knowledge of what to expect and actively wish to attend a performance. If you don't like it — you have been warned!

In fairness I must mention that the universal trend in all art forms against the phony or absolutely outrageous has also extended into opera. New works are being written every year and more and more are becoming easier and easier for audiences to assimilate. For example, Dominick Argento's *Casanova's Homecoming*, based on the old rogue's own memoirs, not only goes back to a three-acts-of-three-scenes-each format and an interesting story developed chronologically, but contains music which fits the subject and period. It may be modern music, but it is far from 'way out'. Premièred in 1985, it is too early to know

91

HOW TO

ENJOY

OPERA

WITHOUT

REALLY

TRYING

whether the latest 'step back' in music, if I can put it that way, will prove to have lasting attraction for the public. I certainly welcome it, as I welcome Menotti, who has been rubbished by his colleagues because for 35 years he has refused to follow them into the atonal sphere. Menotti is modern, but sticks to sound dramatic situations and occasional bursts of Puccini-like melody. No wonder his operas have kept their place in the repertoire. Even so, I would not recommend even Menotti in your early days of opera-going.

# CHAPTER EIGHT

# The Opera Jigsaw

*T*his could, and perhaps should be the beginning of another book, approximately twice as long as what has gone before. Sooner or later, if I have succeeded in what this book attempts, you will want to know more about the huge jigsaw puzzle which is put together each night when an opera is staged. There are a number of books in existence that do all that, but it would not be a bad idea if an inkling could be given of what will be found in detail in those books.

The first thing to realise is that the human voice was never intended to do the things which it is asked to do in operas. You can, of course, say the same thing about rock-'n-roll singing; that is not natural either. But at least the opera singer is restricted by the printed note and his voice must be trained scientifically to obtain the necessary range and tonal quality which the composer demands.

The trouble is that the singing which opera fans find so beguiling that they will pay hundreds of dollars to hear a Pavarotti, Sutherland or Domingo, places an unnatural strain on the voice. It is physically impossible for a leading opera singer to sing every night, let alone eight times a week, as is the case in less strenuous musicals. Some of the latter have become so operatic in musical terms that a show like *Evita* actually ran in major cities with two stars alternating in the title rôle!

*You can't hum the scenery on the way out*, but opera became a mass entertainment when spectacle was added to the singing. Today they can put up — and remove — this Act 2 set from *La Bohème* in ten minutes flat!
(*La Bohème* by Puccini — Metropolitan Opera, New York)

Thus an opera season must change its cast and performance nightly. It is to the credit of administrators world wide that the common practice is to put on a different opera every night. It is simply not possible to double-cast the best operas so that the public is fully satisfied every night. In fact, the best singers will not sing more than twice a week or perhaps three times a fortnight, which would mean more than two casts if the same opera was played every night.

Result: the sets and costumes of whatever plays tonight must be replaced with something else entirely and if matinees as well as evening performances are scheduled on a Saturday or Sunday, the whole thing must be changed twice in one day, only about two hours being available for the change-over. That is not easy, for in the days when these operas were written singers not only sang every night, but scenery was made of painted canvas, while today the public expects solid sets which do not wave in the wind if a door is opened or closed in the course of the action.

Complicated lighting plots have to be changed. The theatre on both sides of the curtain must be cleaned, artists must vacate their dressing rooms, the music must be changed for the orchestra which, in the bigger houses, can number in excess of a hundred, and much more.

To top it all off, the operas to be performed must be rehearsed! And that means, ultimately, rehearsed in full with sets, costumes, lighting, orchestra, the lot. And every part in every opera must have an understudy in case of sudden illness and the understudies cannot do their job unless they also are rehearsed, though they may not get everything with full orchestra as the principals do. The individual members of the orchestra also must have their rehearsal time to become note perfect before the first full rehearsal; orchestral rehearsals are astronomically expensive.

Then the costumes and scenery have firstly to be made and stored, keeping in mind that in any permanent company an opera may remain in the repertoire for at least ten and possibly twenty years, meaning that they have to be made of expensive, durable materials and, in the case of costumes, in such a way that they can be altered (sometimes every week) to suit the figures of singers which can vary from diminutive to enormous. Fortunately the day when costumes and scenery were thrown together

HOW TO

ENJOY

OPERA

WITHOUT

REALLY

TRYING

any old way has long passed. In the 1960s Covent Garden was still using the *Bohème* sets in which Caruso and Melba had sung fifty years earlier and Sir Thomas Beecham, that never-ending mine of provable anecdotes, recounted that one night for a performance of the second act of *Tristan and Isolde* he was astounded to recognise the required castle tower as Big Ben from the current production of Gilbert and Sullivan's *Iolanthe*.

That kind of thing cannot happen in the 1980s and that is why opera is the most expensive art form in the world. One look at the list of staff in a programme shows that hundreds of people are involved, not counting singers or musicians, to get a performance of opera on the stage for a one night stand! No wonder the financial crises facing all major companies occur year after year, if not in London, then in New York or Sydney or Marseilles. The troubles of the funding bodies may not be our concern, but it is worth considering that if there were no subsidies the price of opera tickets could easily equal a week's salary. And that would be the end of opera as an art form.

Final point: if opera is something which is so complicated that so much work has to be done by so many people at such an astronomical cost, and if, for whatever reason, admission to an opera is at a price you can afford, then surely there must be something there worth investigating. And if there is, should you not give it a try?

# *Glossary*

*I*MPORTANT NOTE: It is definitely *not* necessary to read, let alone learn, this Glossary. It is possible that matters relating to opera in the form of reviews, articles or even books may come to the attention of the reader and the following words are likely to be seen and, perhaps, not understood. They include a few words in daily use, such as 'circle' or 'board', which have different meanings among people familiar with opera in its various forms. The Glossary is meant to be consulted, rather than read.

(* = See also alternative entry.)

**Academic:**   A scholar and, theoretically, a promoter of his own speciality, in our case: opera. In the opinion of the author (which is not necessarily shared by everyone) academics can and often do harm their own cause by stressing the value of 'educating' people, of 'learning' about opera. This puts the fear of God into the newcomer. Much can be learned from academics and from their observations about opera, but you can enjoy a good meal without knowing how to cook. The time to seek out the opinion of academics is when you want to know *why* you like opera.

**Accessible:**   Describing music or opera or anything else which readily appeals to the average person.

HOW TO

ENJOY

OPERA

WITHOUT

REALLY

TRYING

***Acoustics:*** The science of sounds. The 'acoustics' of a theatre are good if everybody can hear all sounds produced on the stage as well as in the orchestra pit. Poor acoustics deaden or distort sounds; at worst they even produce an echo so that a single note is actually heard twice. Millions of words have been written by engineers and scientists (and academics) about the best way to build acoustically good opera houses and concert halls. To date nobody has found the secret. Some theatres built hundreds of years ago have perfect acoustics, while some built recently at a cost of millions of dollars have proved their designers so wrong that more millions have had to be spent to re-build world-famous halls. The science of acoustics remains the most unscientific of sciences.

***Acoustic records:*** Recordings made by mechanical means before 'electric' recordings were invented. The generally accepted change-over year is 1925. Acoustic records reproduced the human voice much better than instruments and many thousands made by great singers of the past have been transferred to modern long-playing records. Though invented in the nineteenth century, few records made before 1904 can be enjoyed as more than curiosities.

***Act:*** In operatic terms, the sub-division of a long work by means of intervals. Much confusion reigns today because going to the opera has become a means of enjoying solely the actions on stage. At the time of their creation many operas performed today, whether long or short, were interrupted by many intervals during which much social intercourse took place in the theatre. Time for changing scenery and costumes was also required, and singers of heavy rôles required a break. Today the trend is to fewer intervals and companies often re-number the acts of operas according to the breaks during which the house lights are raised and the audience may leave the auditorium. A simple example will suffice: Verdi wrote *Rigoletto* as a four act opera. The first act is short and the opera has for many, many years been played with only two intervals. Act 1 has become Act 1, Scene* 1, and Act 2 is now Act 1 Scene 2. Interval. Act 3 is called Act 2 Act 4 is Act 3. Even Kobbé's *Complete Opera Book* refers to *Rigoletto* as 'An opera in three acts'. Do not assume that the end of an act means there will be an interval!

***Acting:*** Every opera singer is an actor, but not every actor is an opera singer. For literally centuries opera singers were not required to act at all, only to sing the words which told the story. This has changed dramatically in the twentieth century and it may reasonably be assumed that all singers (even the chorus) will be trained actors. This applies even in early operas which were not written with this kind of treatment in mind. Producers* have invented 'business'* for them to keep the attention of audiences at all times. Their success or failure is sometimes as important as the quality of the singing.

***Aficionado:*** A Spanish word meaning literally 'someone devoted to' this, that or the other. Its most common usage has always been to describe lovers of bull-fights, but in recent years opera-lovers have more and more often been described as *aficionados*. (The bull-fight analogy is sometimes most appropriate!)

***Applause:*** The food for great singing. Unfortunately, it is also the death of opera as music-drama. Some theatres insert specific requests in their printed programmes: 'The public is asked to refrain from interrupting the music with applause', or some other phrase. Composers of serious opera (be they comic, tragic or anything else) have constructed continuous works of musical theatre in an effort to build a romantic mood, or a sense of doom, or the cry to arms. The cult of the singer is at odds with the love of their art. Earlier composers were at the mercy of the star singers, who dictated the terms. Pauses for applause were demanded and still exist in the music. For more than a hundred years the principle has not applied, yet the desire to applaud (encouraged indiscriminately by singers seeking ever higher fees) is as strong as ever. The fact that the whole fabric of what is being witnessed can be destroyed by one clap of the hands is forgotten. Opera is not a sporting event. Intelligent audiences with long traditions of opera-going do not applaud in mid-music. Some do not even do so when an aria is followed by a pause. The fact that somebody

HOW TO

ENJOY

OPERA

WITHOUT

REALLY

TRYING

else has started clapping is no reason to follow like sheep. Newcomers to the art may ponder on this.

**Arena:** Used today solely to describe an open-air venue, usually the ruin of an old Roman circus arena where gladiators fought and chariots raced two thousand years ago. Open spaces often have excellent acoustics* and when a circle of natural land or man-built stone seats lends itself to the presentation of opera, the word 'arena' is used. The most famous one is that in Verona, Italy.

**Aria:** The language of music is historically Italian, as the language of ballet is French. *Aria* mean 'air' in musical terms. Not so many years ago people sang 'airs', rather than 'songs', but the English usage of that word has fallen into disuse. In operas, even English operas, the Italian term *aria* is used to denote a section which is commonly extracted from the whole work and sung as a separate piece of music. It is not a 'tune', but a complete song-like piece of music and exists in a multitude of varieties. Most arias are tuneful enough to be easily assimilated and the number of recognisable arias is a good yardstick by which the popularity of an opera can be judged.

**Aristocracy:** The 'upper classes' created the art form known as opera. It began as the plaything of the noble, later of the rich and only lately of the people, meaning governments.

**Arrangement:** This really means 're-arrangement'. Musically, an 'arrangement' is something which intends to keep the original intact, while improving it. Early operas were seldom written out in full and must be 'arranged' whether you want to or not. Later works were re-arranged, sometimes by the composer himself, in many ways: by cutting, making additions, re-orchestrations, using new words and/or actions, changing the acts or scenes, etc. etc. Theoretically, all arrangements should be an improvement on the original.

**Artistic licence:** Not the kind of licence usually obtained from anyone. It is the right of the interpreter to vary the tempo of the music, the volume or length of a note, to make minor alterations here and there — provided that they keep within the limit of the composer's intentions. When a tenor adds the occasional Top C to an aria in the composer's lifetime, as happened, for example, at the end of 'Di quella pira' in Verdi's *Il trovatore*, the composer may (as Verdi did) say: 'I agree that is good, but you'd better make sure that your Top C remains as good as this all the time.' That is artistic licence which makes sense. Yet for the tenor to follow the soprano to the same note at the closing of the first act of *La Bohème* does not, for it is not in the spirit of the music, nor did Puccini approve it.

**Audience:**   That unpredictable thing without which opera cannot and will not prosper or even exist. The approval or disapproval of a full or half-empty theatre is what opera is all about. The behaviour of a few can spoil the pleasure of many. Applause* can do as much harm as booing*, if it comes in the wrong place or is prompted by the wrong motives. Applauders and booers alike have been paid by rival singers, and managers as well. Some cities are notorious for the behaviour of their audiences, others are dreaded by singers for their politeness which gives moderate praise to the good, bad and mediocre alike. There have been rare instances when performances have been met with total silence. Even that can be misunderstood. A truly great performance can grip an audience so much that at its final curtain applause comes only slowly after what could be said to be a very pregnant pause. Applause which builds is more genuine than an instant standing ovation, which can be engineered by the management, singers, partisans or a paid *claque**. So can masses of flowers, streamers and shrill whistles of approval. Booing is often self-defeating; it encourages those who disagree to applaud all the louder. Yet both involve audience participation and that is better than polite approval.

**Auditorium:**   The part of a building housing the audience. Ideally it should have good acoustics* and perfect sight-lines*. In Europe these factors are taken into consideration when tickets are sold; some theatres have twenty different prices for seats, according to their quality. Elsewhere only minor price variations

HOW TO

ENJOY

OPERA

WITHOUT

REALLY

TRYING

occur, the bulk of the seats, regardless of sight-lines, cost the same, the most the traffic will carry. Some of the world's greatest theatres have very poor auditoriums. Unfortunately, they also pay the highest fees to their artists. The result is a negation of all that has made opera greater in recent times: people pay to hear singers sing, no more. If you can't see properly, all their efforts to portray rôles well in magnificent settings go for nought.

***Avant-garde:*** A term used in the French army for the front line, the leading troop of soldiers. In music, art and opera it is the explorer of new territory. Once upon a time people were clamouring to hear the latest works by the new as well as old-established composers. Everybody hoped to discover the next Verdi or Puccini. Alas, no more. Yet we can not afford to stand still. Experimentations with music and production techniques can go (and have gone) about as far as they can go. Something must follow, if the art is not to die. The *avant-garde* fills that need and must be encouraged. Let us not forget that for every Verdi or Wagner there were hundreds of long forgotten innovators whose ideas did not work, while those of the remembered ones did. Many of the most popular works today were abject failures at their premières. Who today can predict which, if any, *avant-garde* composer will be the Puccini of 2086?

***Baritone:*** The natural voice of most men, covering the middle range in which they speak. (See also 'Voice'.)

***Baroque:*** An early period of music roughly covering the seventeenth and eighteenth centuries, i.e. the period in which great advances were made in musical development and also in opera. Handel was the greatest composer of baroque operas. The period ended with the arrival of Mozart.

***Bass:*** The deepest and rarest male voice, which requires some inborn natural resonance which can not be created artificially. A baritone can be taught to sing higher notes, but it is almost impossible to turn him into a *basso profundo*, who can produce the deepest and often most beautifully rounded low notes. (See also Voice.)

**Bass-baritone:**  A baritone with a good, but limited, lower range. He can sing bass as well as baritone parts. The majority of basses are really bass-baritones. (See also 'Voice'.)

**Bel canto:**  A much misused phrase. Translates as 'beautiful singing'. Describes the finely spun singing method supposedly practised in the early nineteenth century, traces of which can be heard on some early recordings. In reality a meaningless term, since nobody knows what true *bel canto* sounded like.

**Billing:**  The subject of much dispute in every aspect of the theatrical arts but, curiously enough, rarely today in opera. While star singers are still the biggest box office attractions, they are usually listed in alphabetical order, women first and then the men. It may avoid arguments among the stars but can be confusing to anyone unfamiliar with the singers. Small part players whose names start with A, B, or C are listed before Domingo or Pavarotti.

**Blood and thunder:**  A common description of very highly dramatic plots and/or music. By no means is it a condemnation in operatic terms; a majority of the most popular operas fall into this category, which covers every form of melodrama, anything involving violence, murder and the like. Few art forms contain more blood and thunder than opera.

**Board:**  In opera literature this means 'board of directors'.

**Booing:**  The hooting sound most commonly used by an audience to show its disapproval. Hissing like snakes is equally effective, though less commonly used in English-speaking countries, where it is usually aimed at other members of the audience, to silence them. Most confusing of all is whistling, which is utter condemnation in one place and highest praise in others. The universal language everywhere is 'boo' for dis-approval and 'bravo' for approval. (Snobs like to be specific and shout '*brava*' to the soprano and '*bravi*' to the whole cast.)

103

HOW TO

ENJOY

OPERA

WITHOUT

REALLY

TRYING

**Book:**   The common term used for the complete libretto* of an opera, not including the music, of course.

**Box office:**   Both the small room from which tickets are sold and also the term used to describe the takings. A 'box office opera' is one which sells a lot of tickets.

**Bread and butter:**   'Reliable'. You can always count on certain operas which will attract an audience large enough to cover costs. They are the 'bread and butter' of the annual budget. The 'box office operas' are the jam.

**Business:**   You can do good business at the box office. But on a stage 'business' mean doing things, not exactly 'busy-ness', but the actions done by singers which are non-musical, the picking up of a book, the pinching of a bottom, tripping on a stair — anything which helps the action is classed as 'business'. ('Giving somebody the business' is not an expression used in opera, except perhaps in American theatres.)

**Cadenza:**   The section of an aria in which the orchestra stops and the singer is supposed to improvise elaborations on the music being sung. In the early days of operas there were literally singing contests on the stage in which two singers competed with each other to see who could produce more complicated cadenzas. Only since the days of Rossini (the nineteenth century!) have cadenzas been fully written out by composers who were fed up with the lack of taste of the famous singers of their day.

**Castrato:**   The earliest singing stars in opera were the *castrati* (the plural form of *castrato*). Women were not allowed on stage and men sang all the parts, female as well as male. A normal man can only sing high notes with a method known as *falsetto*, literally a 'false voice'. Castrating boy sopranos before their voices broke, produced some 'castrated men' who retained genuine soprano singing voices of extraordinary power and agility. The fame of the star *castrati* was greater than that of any singer known today. The penalty they paid was, of course, the loss of their masculinity and the practice died out during the nineteenth century. The last known castrato died as recently as 1921, but he was a member of the Choir of the Sistine Chapel and never sang in opera. *Castrato* rôles are usually sung by contraltos today.

***Censor:*** The censor plays a very important rôle in opera, not as a guardian of our morals, but as a political commissar. Operas were produced in countries governed by monarchs or occupied by foreign powers. They were easily, and sometimes deliberately, used to satirise royalty or to encourage insurrection. In one historical instance, a country (Belgium in 1830) became independent as a result of a revolution started by a riot during an opera, Auber's *La Muette de Portici.* Censors had to pass all operas before they were performed and influenced every aspect of performances, as they did once again in this century on the orders of Hitler and Stalin.

***Chest voice:*** The lower register of the human voice. ('Middle' and 'head' voice* are the others.) Very unfashionable at present, because it is considered unfeminine, the chest voice was used by all three female voices extensively during the Golden Age of Opera, especially by dramatic sopranos and contraltos. Suppression of the almost baritonal growling of the register can only be done at the cost of losing the resonance of the natural voice. As a result the lower voices sound like sopranos* without a top and the true contralto* has all but disappeared.

***Chamber opera:*** As in 'chamber music', an opera for a small ensemble of singers with few instruments or a piano accompanying it.

***Chorus:*** In the antique sense, which is used in a few operas, it is the man, woman or multiple of both who comment on the action in Greek drama. The more common usage of the term 'chorus' applies to the mass of singers who do not have individual identifiable parts in the plot of an opera.

***Circle:*** 'Dress Circle', 'Grand Circle' and various other varieties of 'Circle' are the seats higher than the ground floor in a theatre.

HOW TO

ENJOY

OPERA

WITHOUT

REALLY

TRYING

They are usually arranged in a half circle to give each patron a direct sight-line\* of the stage, hence the term 'circle'.

***Claque:*** A group of audience\* members, usually in the cheapest seats, who are often paid by singers or their rivals to start applause for or a demonstration against some individual taking part in the performance. The heads of *claques* can become very powerful personages, who call on new artists to demand free tickets and money to ensure their success. Theoretically, *claques* are dying out — managements frown on them — but indications are that they are alive and well and living largely in Italian and German opera houses.

***Classical:*** A meaningless term, mostly used by musical illiterates to describe music they can not or do not want to understand. There is no such thing as 'classical music' or even 'good music', because nobody has ever been able to draw a distinction where, how or why something is classical and something else is not. It is a matter of what a person likes or what follows certain academic specifications. All composers, even a Beethoven or Mozart, write some bad as well as good music. Yet the bad also must be termed 'classical' if the word is to mean anything, which it does not.

***Cliché:*** Something which has been done so often before that you can see it coming. Due to the demands of singers in the past operas are full of musical *clichés*; for example, a tenor aria\* is often followed by a fast, rousing *coda*\*, ending with a ringing top note, to raise a storm of applause.

***Climax:*** Musically and dramatically every opera is a mounting series of climaxes, if it has any lasting value. In these terms a climax can be an enormous ensemble of singers bringing the house down, e.g. the Grand March in *Aida*, or a death in which not a single note is sung, as in the final scene of *La Bohème*. The more climaxes, the more popular an opera. Mood pieces, like Debussy's *Pelléas and Melisande*, can be great emotional experiences, but they rarely count for much at the box office.

**Coda:**  A piece added to the end of an aria* or ensemble* whose purpose is almost always the attraction of applause. Codas to many famous arias used to be omitted as a matter of course in theatres and recordings until recent years, because they do not usually advance the action, and can be a hazard for the singer's voice. The present vogue for 'complete' performances has restored the *coda* to its rightful place and, particularly in the case of Verdi's operas, it has often been found that they form an essential bridge in the dramatic action. A notable example is the *coda* to Alfredo's aria in the second act of *La Traviata*. Without it the tenor simply leaves the stage for no discernible reason.

**Coloratura:**  Not a type of singer, but a kind of music, namely the florid ornamentations of runs and trills for which light sopranos in particular are ideally suited. However, every kind of voice, even the deepest bass, has coloratura passages to sing in some rôles. One part of coloratura, the ability to trill, has almost disappeared. Fortunately, coloratura is found mostly in cadenzas* or improvisiations. Alteration to it (in the spirit of the music) is not considered a sin.

**Comedy:**  Something which is supposed to make us laugh, but in opera it can have many other meanings. *Don Giovanni* is described by Mozart as a *dramma giocoso*, a funny drama. A good producer can stage Mozart's masterpiece as a humorous drama. After all, Don Giovanni doesn't get any of his women — he is frustrated on every side. *The Marriage of Figaro* is a farce; a farce with glorious music, but a farce just the same. And let us not forget that what was once considered funny is not funny to us today. People went to lunatic asylums to laugh at the inmates! Sometimes opera offers comedy which is not funny and drama which is.

**Commercials:**  Perhaps not part of opera, but opera is very much a part of television commercials. A good tune will sell any product and opera is full of good tunes. No television viewer can fail to know any number of operatic extracts!

107

HOW TO

ENJOY

OPERA

WITHOUT

REALLY

TRYING

***Composer:*** The man who above all is responsible for the success of any opera. Too many operas suffer from the most abysmal librettos*, yet stay in the repertoire* on the strength of their music. Yet even the composer who is his own master, who chooses his own librettist* and his own story, must have the text before he writes his music. No opera has ever been written for which the words were added afterwards. An opera composer is inspired by the word. He can write good music for bad words and he can write bad music to good words. Opera is drama with music, not music with drama. The fact that the music, not the words, make it immortal does not alter this fact.

***Conductor:*** The one thing wrong with the famous film *Amadeus* was that it showed Mozart conducting his own operas. The conductor* came much later, in the nineteenth century, when orchestras* grew so large that an independent leader was needed to keep the players together. Mozart and all those before him and many of those who followed him (including Beethoven) conducted from the harpsichord or the piano or, less often, by playing the first violin. Today the conductor is the central figure in an opera performance. He not only conducts, he casts the singers and acts as overall artistic director of the work on which he is engaged.

***Contemporary music:*** Music written at the present time. After a while all music ceases to be contemporary. Every composer wrote contemporary music, music of his own time. Good, bad or indifferent, it influenced and influences those who came or will come later.

***Contralto:*** The lowest of the female voices, which in past centuries was considered the most desirable — possibly in the reaction against the high *castrato** voices which began to disappear in the eighteenth century. The deep chesty growl of a good contralto is a rarity today, because the great female stars of the twentieth century were all sopranos.* The intermediate voice (the female equivalent of the baritone) is the mezzo soprano* and most contraltos like to be known by that more glamorous title in our time. What is completely overlooked is that the best contraltos have excellent high notes; some can go to top C with ease. True contraltos are factually sopranos or mezzo-sopranos with a resonant lower register, i.e. they have a lower range than their competitors. The reason why they probably consider themselves inferior may be based on the fact that few leading rôles (e.g. Delilah in *Samson and Delilah* or Azucena in *Il trovatore*) require the chest voice*, which is frowned on by critics who should know better. Sopranos, and even mezzos, who use their natural deep range are positively reviled for doing what comes naturally. With luck there will be a reversal to earlier practices, as happened temporarily in the 1920s when Conchita Supervia sang the Rossini heroines in their original contralto key. Unfortunately, the truly great contralto voice of Clara Butt (1873–1936) is today used as the butt (pun intended) of female impersonators of the opposite gender.

***Conventions:*** Operatic conventions can change almost annually, by the decade and almost always in a century. What is fashionable today may be laughable tomorrow, and vice versa. Conventions are so numerous that it is impossible to list even a selection. Let one recent glaring example only be quoted: in the 1920s and 1930s the light lyric coloratura soprano was considered the ultimate in artistry. Singers like Galli-Curci and Lily Pons were the highest paid stars. The fact that they starred in music written for chesty contraltos, such as Rosina in *The Barber of Seville* mattered not at all. After World War II dramatic sopranos like Tebaldi and Callas became the fashion and mezzo sopranos* sang Rosina. Here today and gone tomorrow applies to literally hundreds of different aspects of the operatic art.

***Costumes:*** Clothes worn by singers in opera, as they are by actors in plays. They can be of any period, past, present or future, but should be in keeping with those of others appearing in the same work. Long ago stars were expected to provide their own costumes and many insist on doing so to this day. This practice can result in ludicrous anomalies. No overall design can ever be maintained if any part of it can be changed at the whim of a singer. Modern designers and their audiences expect reasonable visual harmony in an opera production. One unfortunate

HOW TO

ENJOY

OPERA

WITHOUT

REALLY

TRYING

by-product of this natural process is that some very expensive costumes have to be duplicated when a rôle created by a diminutive singer is taken over by a very large, but equally famous, star. The generally accepted middle path is a costume which can be taken in or let out in every direction. Only the biggest box office* draws can afford to insist on brand new costumes when appearing in existing productions.

**Countertenor:**  An unusual, but natural, male voice which can be mistaken for a contralto or even a soprano, though the quality of the sound is such as to make an actual impersonation unreal. Few rôles in operas are written for countertenors (Oberon in Benjamin Britten's *A Midsummer-Night's Dream* is one), but the voice is often used in productions of older operas when the music has been written for *castrati** or contraltos* cast as men.

**Critics:**  Writers who are always wrong in somebody's eyes. Their opinions can and do affect audience attendances, but they happen to be human, are far from infallible and their opinions of one opera, one singer or one performance can produce completely opposing views. The greatest composers have been adversely criticised and the most obscure praised to the skies. People will always want to hear or read the opinions of 'experts', but criteria vary as fashions and/or conventions* vary. No critic is always right, but some are always wrong. Which has not yet stopped publishers from printing their opinions.

**Criticism:**  The term has quite wrongly become identified with adverse commentary. To 'criticise' means 'to pass an opinion' on something or the other. Praise is as valid as condemnation in defining criticism.

**Critique:**  A fancy name for the review of an opera or anything else. If you use a French word instead of an English one, the opinion of the writer is more valid. Or so some people believe.

**Curtain:**  The word has a double meaning in stage (or opera) language. It accurately describes the hanging cloth which covers the proscenium arch of a theatre before and after an act or the whole performance. Yet a 'final curtain' can refer to a production in which no curtain is ever used; it describes the end of something, and singers may take 'curtain calls' in an open-air arena in which no scenery of any kind appears.

**Designers:**  The artists who are responsible for the stage picture. Originally they actually painted the scenery and were given credit for that on playbills and in programmes. Economic necessity caused their anonymity in most nineteenth century companies, which had a stock of back-cloths and costumes, to be brought out to suit the opera being presented, at times with ludicrous results. Though we may never reach the point when designers will be the most important people in opera, their work can make or break a production today. The overall 'stage picture', involving scenery*, costumes* and props*, should blend with the actions of the singers as well as the music they sing. Some of the best producers of opera are also their own designers, but a truly great visual artist is seldom endowed with the ability to direct singers in their performance of an opera.

**Dialogue:**  Unaccompanied spoken words ('dialogue'), or sung speech (*'recitative'*) or words with a musical background (*'melodrama'*).

**Director:**  There is considerable disputation about this title. In opera it means the same as 'producer', a term which in films and theatre can have quite a different meaning. Both terms are used to describe the man who is in charge of the stage action, who tells the singers what to do in all things which are not musical: movement, facial expression, entries and exits, the use of props.* A director 'directs' his singers to do everything which is necessary to realise the dramatic content of an opera. He also should correlate the designing and lighting of the production with the actions of the performers. He and the conductor — who is the musical 'director', not the musical 'producer' — are as important as the singers and the orchestra in staging the musical drama we call opera.

111

HOW TO

ENJOY

OPERA

WITHOUT

REALLY

TRYING

**Double-bill:**  Two short operas which together make up one full evening of opera.

**Drama:**  The word covering the complexities of presenting a story in visual terms. Reading a story is not a drama. Acting it out on a stage, with different actors or singers playing each part, is. A musical drama, a drama with music, is an opera.

**Duet:**  Arias involving more than one singer are simple multiples, i.e. duet, trio, quartet, quintet, sextet, etc. Every opera contains varieties of these, some of which are so famous that you don't even have to name the title of the piece. The *Rigoletto quartet* or the *Lucia sextet* is enough!

**Electric recording:**  All records made after 1925 were recorded electrically, but the term is only applied to historical recordings made between that date and the appearance of long-playing records about 1950.

**Electronic music:**  Produced by computers, synthesisers and other instruments, it creates sounds through electric impulses rather than acoustic, let alone vocal, methods. Electronic effects or accompaniments appear in a number of modern operas and a very few actually use electronic sounds in place of the human voice. None to date has succeeded in replacing the vocal cords of the human throat.

**Encore:**  A strange word, supposedly French, but probably based on the Italian 'ancora' (again). An encore is a repeat of an aria due to audience demand. It is very rare today outside Italy. Both French and Italian audiences call for encores by crying '*bis*'. Perhaps it is better for singers to be 'encored' than 'bissed'.

**Ensemble:**  A collection of things. In opera it can apply to a small orchestra or any number of singers. Nobody knows why a hundred voices make an 'ensemble', while a hundred instru-mentalists are an 'orchestra'. A set piece for more than two singers can also be called an 'ensemble'.

**Extra:**   A non-singing character in an opera who is not an individual. More often than not, a soldier carrying a spear, but he or she could be any kind of character. By mixing extras with chorus singers, the audience can be fooled into believing the ensemble\* is bigger than the budget allows.

**Falsetto:**   A 'faked' note in the upper range of the voice. It is very weak and can rarely be used legitimately to enhance the music. Used mainly by singers with a limited range, or to imitate women if the action calls for it. Not to be mistaken for 'head voice'\*.

**Festival:**   The name given to almost any special occasion which involves music. Because it is the most expensive art form, most festivals include one or more operas, usually staged by a visiting opera company. Wagner's own theatre in Bayreuth is called the *Festspielhaus*, Festival Theatre, and its seasons are known as the Bayreuth Festival.

**Fiasco:**   A disastrous failure, but not necessarily a fatal one. *La traviata* was described by Verdi as a *fiasco* after its première.

**Films:**   Old, recent and new films have been and are responsible for much falsification of musical history; unfortunately true life stories are seldom entertaining in a continuous sense. However, films have also created a large following for opera by starring singers and exposing millions to music from operas. No opera composed for a film has ever been completed. (A few written for television survive, notably Menotti's *Amahl and the Night Visitors*.) Existing operas have been adapted for the cinema with limited success or simply filmed in opera houses in actual performance. Even the best opera films lack the excitement which can be created in a live performance. Not only seeing, but hearing is believing and no way has yet been found to improve on the real thing, a fact which is readily proved by audiences who attend the same opera, often with the same singers, again and again. At best, filmed opera enables people to see singers and productions they are unable to see and hear in the flesh.

HOW TO

ENJOY

OPERA

WITHOUT

REALLY

TRYING

**Finale:**   Obviously, an ending. But finales in opera occur at the end of most acts and even scenes. They are usually musical highlights of the work.

**Forte:**   Musical term indicating loudness. *Fortissimo* is very loud.

**Funding:**   One of the most commonly used words in newspaper stories about opera companies today. Because the art form itself began as the plaything of the high, mighty or rich, and because it combines more components than any other art, it is impossible to stage an opera season which can survive on the sale of tickets alone. Funds must be donated from private or public purses to enable opera companies to survive. In Europe it is not unusual for such funding by the state to reach 85% of the total cost of running an opera company. In some countries private and corporate donors usually add to any state subsidies, while in America many companies survive on private sponsorship alone. If no funding were available, tickets to one first-class opera would cost in the region of an average week's wage in the currency of the theatre's country.

**Gallery:**   A theatre's highest balcony or circle of seats, usually occupied by not only the poorest, but also the most knowledgeable and most demonstrative section of the audience. In many countries it is also the most corruptible. (See '*Claque*').

**Gimmick:**   Any special trick which attracts attention. Clever gimmicks can add greatly to production values. Gimmicks which misfire can ruin a performance. Staging an opera in a period other than that intended by the composer is the most popular gimmick of producers today. Successes and failures balance about evenly in this field.

**Grand opera:**   A specific form of opera, not just an opera with a very large cast. It refers to opera as performed in France in the mid-nineteenth century and its specific points of reference: an historical story on an epic scale in four or five acts, a ballet which

114

had to be in the middle act, etc. 'Grand Opera Seasons' imply that all serious opera is 'grand opera'. This is not so.

**Harmony:**   In layman's language, music pleasing to the ear. Unfortunately, what pleases one ear may not please another. Musical science has ways of defining the technical distinction between right and wrong in harmonic structure. Beethoven and Wagner were two composers who were abused for writing un-harmonious music. You may draw your own conclusions.

**Head voice:**   Not to be mistaken for *falsetto**, but a way of singing high notes very softly, giving the impression that the note is produced in the head. Once the standard way of singing top notes*, it is only used today for special effects, mainly in some French operas.

**Hissing:**   See 'Booing'

**Incidental Music:**   Originally provided for most plays, it is comparable to the background music found in films and television. The great composers of the past wrote it on commission and many forgotten plays have been immortalised by their music. (Beethoven's *Coriolanus* music was not written for Shakespeare's play, but for one by someone called Collin and the original for which Schubert wrote his *Rosamunde* music cannot even be found!) In opera incidental music should be part of a continuous sound picture, but in many cases it is used to accompany speech, *recitative** or stage action which is not sung.

**Intermezzo:**   An orchestral piece played between scenes,* sometimes to suggest the passage of time while the curtain* is up.

**Interval:**   A break in the action during which the audience may leave the auditorium*, as opposed to pauses between scenes*, or even acts*, during which the curtain* is lowered and the house lights are only partly raised.

HOW TO

ENJOY

OPERA

WITHOUT

REALLY

TRYING

***Introduction:*** The beginning of an opera, act\* or even aria\* which is played by the orchestra to set the mood. Hardly ever a separate piece of music.

***Kitsch:*** A German word describing something which is in bad taste or artificially enhanced for no other reason than financial gain. Bad art is considered *Kitsch*. However, since there is no definition of what is good or bad in art or music, there has recently been a vogue for *Kitsch*; it has became an art form in itself. Opera houses today schedule works which academics have condemned in the past as *Kitsch*!

***Kitchen sink:*** Like *Kitsch*, this is a description of an art form. It became fashionable after World War II. Named after plays which were set in current times and people's homes and kitchens. It is a modern variant of opera's *verismo*\*, although (due to its much more recent origins) no operas of this type have yet achieved the fame of 'kitchen sink' plays.

***Legend:*** Another term which has at least two distinct meanings in opera. The literal 'legends', which have come down in history, have been used frequently as the subject of some very popular operas. At the same time, 'legend' and 'legendary' are commonly used as the highest form of praise for singers, some of whom become 'legends in their own lifetimes'.

***Leitmotiv:*** 'Leading motive' or 'theme tune'. A musical phrase identified with a character, object or action. Not invented by Wagner, though its most complex, yet also most obvious, use occurs in his *Ring des Nibelungen*. See also Page 82.

***Libretto:*** The words of an opera or, to a lesser degree, its story. A good libretto says a lot with very few words. If it is adaptation of an existing literary or theatrical work, it should condense the action to a minimum; time is required for the music to develop. An ideal example is Verdi's *Otello*, which takes Shakespeare's play, eliminates five characters completely, yet uses key portions of Shakespeare's own text, if in translation. Only a single aria (Iago's 'Creed') does not appear in the play *Othello*.

***Librettist:*** He gets a separate entry, because the work involved in creating an opera libretto* can be done in many different ways. Ideally it should be the work of the composer himself, e.g. Wagner wrote all his texts. More commonly it is a collaboration between the composer and poet or writer. Many of the best operas have two librettists, one to write the story and the other to versify it; it is easier to write a good tune if the words rhyme. Other variants exist; multiple collaborations, in which contributors sometimes depart in mid-composition and are replaced. It can reach the point that no librettist is mentioned at all. In the case of Puccini's *Manon Lescaut* listing the *seven* men who contributed substantially to the end result in any order of preference would have been impossible.

***Liebestod:*** A German word which has entered the English vocabulary because it describes in one word something which is difficult to explain. The actual *Liebestod* is the death of Isolde in *Tristan and Isolde* by Wagner. She dies, or fades away, because her lover is dead. A close association of love and death was fashionable in the nineteenth century and dying of or for love, without suffering injury or disease, was considered most romantic. (Suicide for love ran a poor second.)

***Lighting:*** A comparatively recent innovation in all types of theatre is the use of complex lighting. Until the beginning of this century the lights were kept on in theatres during performances, making even the illusion of night and day difficult on the other side of the footlights. Today many productions* do away with scenery* altogether, relying entirely on lighting effects, but even the simplest kind of lighting has become a science. The lighting designer more and more often is given credit in the printed programme together with the conductor*, producer* and the singers.

***Literature:*** The vast majority of operas are based on some literary work, be it a play or a book or a poem. A good opera needs a good plot and a good libretto*. You can not treat opera purely on its musical merits. On rare occasions composers will create operas which are figments of their own imagination.

HOW TO

ENJOY

OPERA

WITHOUT

REALLY

TRYING

Wagner is again the most famous example, though he drew on many sources for his inspiration. This only proves that some composers have literary talents: Wagner learned to write music to assist in the realisation of his epic poems. He was a writer first and a musician later. Every one of his librettos received public readings before a note of the music was composed!

***Lyrics:***   The words to songs, strictly speaking, particularly in musicals and operas with spoken dialogue. A lyricist is not necessarily the librettist\*, though the two can be combined in one person.

***Mad scene:***   Second only to love-death (*Liebestod*\*) dramatically, 'mad scenes' in opera proliferated among nineteenth-century starring vehicles for singers. A mad heroine could rattle away at any kind of vocal gyrations without the need to justify the composer's music. For a time there was hardly an opera without a mad scene — or more than one! Bellini's *I Puritani* has no less than three, all sung by the same heroine.

***Masonry:***   It is natural that famous composers should be invited to become masons, members of the once powerful secret society of important people who could make or break a celebrity. Many composers, notably Mozart, made references to masonry in their operas, but their existence and meaning neither adds nor detracts from the value of the works in which they appear.

***Melodrama:***   Nothing whatever to do with the plots of operas, which are often very melodramatic indeed, the term 'melodrama' is used to describe spoken dialogue which is accompanied by music, but not spoken in time with it.

***Melody:***   A tune, but not a song or aria\* or piece of music, only that section of it which sounds melodious.

***Mezzo:***   Italian: halfway, the middle. A qualification of another term. *Forte* (loud) become *mezzo-forte* if it is not very loud. *Mezza voce* means using only half the voice, not singing full out. A low soprano or a high contralto\* becomes a *mezzo-soprano*\* if the natural middle of the voice lies between the two. Also used as an abbreviation of mezzo-soprano.

***Mezzo-soprano:*** The mid-range female voice, strongest in the centre, but lacking the highest notes of the true soprano* and the lowest of the true contralto*. The female equivalent of the male baritone. (See also Voice.)

***Modern music:*** See 'Contemporary music'.

***Multi-purpose:*** Opera is a complex medium and most parts can be adapted to suit more than one purpose, usually for reasons of economy. Multi-purpose sets are the most common. A good designer can produce a basic set* which, by the addition of various minor components can reproduce artistically satisfying entities which are, on the face of it, not compatible, e.g. a garden can be transformed into a room.

***Music theatre:*** A specific term used to describe a new concept of opera which is not used to show off singers, but to enhance a realistic or abstract stage attraction through the medium of music. Some experiments in this field have actually been staged without any singers at all, while others have had major symphonic works incorporated in their action. Music theatre rarely has a continuous story line. It is always experimental and decidedly modern.

***Musical:*** As a noun the term is applied to modern musical stage plays in which the musical items are insertions in a dramatic narrative, i.e. the drama is the principal motivation, not the music. *My Fair Lady* without the music would be an approximation of G. B. Shaw's *Pygmalion*, on which it is based. When the music of a musical is very good, and/or better than the story line, the work is often performed by opera companies.

***Musical comedy:*** The predecessor of the musical, it is similar in structure, but its music does not demand particularly good voices. Actors, like Noël Coward, more or less speaking the

HOW TO

ENJOY

OPERA

WITHOUT

REALLY

TRYING

songs, used to play the leading rôles. Musical comedy is unlikely to be seen in an opera house.

**Musical director:**   Not necessarily the conductor*, though the position is frequently held by the principal conductor of an opera company. The musical director is responsible for every aspect of the musical side of an opera season, both in the pit* and on the stage*.

**Musicologist:**   Someone who studies music or advances its cause through the scientific exploration of its aspects in books. Rarely a performer.

**Mythology:**   The exploration of ancient legends and myths, most of which used to be the subject of musical interpretation in early operas, and some more recent ones. Once a standard subject taught in schools, mythology lent itself to satire, resulting in comic operas and operettas* by composers like Offenbach.

**Nordic:**   Read: Scandinavian as much as German. The ancient religions of cold northern Europe were not left to posterity in written detail as were those of Greece or Rome. As a consequence German composers* trying to draw on their own legends* were forced to invent figures and/or gods who in Mediterranean countries had positive identities. All the Wagnerian heroes and villains are conglomerations of many mythical characters of uncertain origin.

**Notes:**   The individual tones — sung, played or written — which make up any kind of music.

**Number:**   Although operas are sub-divided numerically by their composers, and used in this way during rehearsals, the use of the word 'number' to describe a part of an opera is considered a sign of ignorance. Pop singers sing 'numbers'. Opera singers sing arias* or extracts or even 'that bit in the second act'. Never 'a number'.

***Opening:***   The beginning of an act*, scene* or musical item.

***Opera:***   Literally, Italian for any kind of action or work. Musically, it can mean an immense variety of things, the principal and most popular being an entertaining play in which the actors sing their words instead of speaking them.

***Opéra comique:***   Not at all what the words imply. A comic opera can be an *opéra comique*, but *opéra comique* is not a comic opera. The term originated in nineteenth century Paris where the Opéra played through-composed operas, without spoken dialogue, while the theatre called Opéra-Comique played works in which the music was interrupted by, often very brief, spoken sections. Beethoven's *Fidelio* and Bizet's *Carmen* are *opéras comiques* and the theatre from which the name came premièred some of the most serious works in today's repertoire.

***Opera house:***   The title is borne by a large number of buildings which are far from suitable for the presentation of opera. Having an opera house has always been considered a matter of civic pride and the title is really meaningless. A good opera house should have a large orchestra pit and a larger than usual stage, which immediately rules out the most famous building in the world bearing that name, the magnificent sculpture in Australia known as the Sydney Opera House.

***Operetta:***   One of the few words in the Glossary which actually means what it says. An operetta is a small opera*, usually (but not always) a comedy with bright tunes and spoken dialogue. Many operettas have long ago been accepted into the repertoire of major opera houses and, as time passes, others are constantly being added.

***Orchestra:***   There are three very different meanings to the word 'orchestra'. In ancient Greece it was the area between the audience and the stage where, due to the lack of back-stage facilities, members of the cast sat while waiting their turn to participate in the action. From this arose the practice of calling the front seats of the ground floor (the stalls*) 'the orchestra'. Yet

121

HOW TO

ENJOY

OPERA

WITHOUT

REALLY

TRYING

even in theatres where this is done, the term 'orchestra' is also used as the name for the bulk of instrumentalists who play as an ensemble* in the 'pit'* or on a concert platform. A good orchestra in a first-class opera house should have about one hundred players.

***Original scores:*** Only during the past thirty years has the practice of going back to the original scores of composers become the norm, a norm which cannot be and is not enforced. The aim to produce exactly what the creator intended is admirable, but composers themselves changed their minds, added, subtracted and altered their scores to suit circumstances, often in a deliberate attempt to improve their first thoughts. There can be no strict adherence to any such rule, unless the composer is still alive. And how many different versions of major works by living composers are there? More than a few!

***Overture:*** An ambiguous word, historically; once upon a time it meant the same as 'symphony'. In opera the overture is played before the first scene of the first act. Not all overtures belong to the work which they precede (e.g. that to *The Barber of Seville* was used by Rossini for no less than four different operas; the real *Barber* overture is lost) and some bear little relation to what follows. The most common is a pot-pourri of tunes from the work whose name it bears, preparing the audience for pleasures to come.

***Pantomime:*** Strictly speaking, wordless actions. In practical terms, the kind of Christmas musical play intended for children, which is now falling into disuse. In opera there are numerous principal rôles which are taken by dancers, actors or mimes who do not utter any sound; they mime their parts. Some operas contains parts in which a singer is forced to remain silent for a whole act or more; the love duet in Dvořák's *Rusalka* is sung by the tenor alone!

***Patrons:*** Either the customers who have paid for their seats or the donors of funds who 'patronise' the art in return for social glory, commercial advertising or the pleasure they get by being

associated with a thing they love. Opera needs both kinds. (See
also 'Funding'.)

***Piano:***   Italian for 'soft'; *pianissimo* for 'very soft'. The best
singers are judged by their ability to sing softly. Anyone with a
good natural voice* can sing loudly; it is the artistry of con-
trolling not only the quality but the volume of the voice which
distinguishes a good singer from a bad one. Piano is also short for
pianoforte, an instrument rarely used in opera performances.

***Pit:***   The orchestra pit in front of the stage is the subject of
endless, if rarely public, arguments. Logically, Wagner had the
right idea when he built his own theatre in Bayreuth. Only there
is the orchestra completely hidden from the audience's* view.
Elsewhere the vanity of conductors and players alike expose the
orchestra fully, making it so prominent that singers are drowned
and delicate lighting effects on stage ruined. No solution is in
sight. (In England the cheapest back stalls are referred to as 'the
pit'.)

***Pitch:***   The accuracy of a sung or played note. To vary the pitch
of a note slightly is the worst crime a singer can commit. Being
'flat' (just under the note) is considered worse than being 'sharp'
(just above the note). Either way, the note and everything before
and after it sounds wrong and is wrong.

***Piece:***   Better than 'number'*, but no singer or musician is
flattered to be told that he sang or played a 'piece' from this or
that opera.

***Plot:***   Not only the story of an opera, but the way things are
done. The 'lighting plot', for example, is the complicated programme which lists positions of all lamps and the cues for their
use, their brightness, colour, etc. etc.

***Politics:***   What have politics to do with opera, apart from
providing tax-payers' money? See under 'Censor'.

HOW TO

ENJOY

OPERA

WITHOUT

REALLY

TRYING

***Prelude:*** The overture to an opera or a scene* of an opera, or both.

***Première:*** Normally, the first performance of any work, but usable in distorted form by good publicity agents to promote almost any opera in which anything from singers to production may happen to be new.

***Pretentious:*** Not necessarily something which pretends to be something which it is not, but rather something over-ambitious intended to reflect credit on some thing or person. Cannot be used in any way as flattery.

***Prima donna:*** The now meaningless description of a soprano* who sings leading rôles. (The male equivalent is *primo uomo.*) Over-promotion has made every singer a prima donna and every dancer a ballerina. Both terms strictly should mean the *one* lady who is the undisputed star of a specific opera company, season or performance. Nobody can be a prima donna while not engaged to sing under contract.

***Principal:*** A singer engaged to sing leading rôles.

***Producer:*** See 'Director'

***Production:*** The overall result of the non-musical efforts of hundreds of people working on an opera* under the direction of the producer/director*.

***Program(me):*** A once clear separation has become confused through the use of the American standard 'program' for all things programmatic. Two things are involved, the programme for a season of opera which is planned and executed, and the programme which is printed and given or sold to the audience.

***Props:*** Short for 'properties', any object in an opera which is not part of the set*, but can be moved by the singers or used by them, e.g. swords, crockery, food, jewellery, etc.

**Quartet:**  See 'Duet'.

**Quintet:**  See 'Duet'.

**Range:**  The upper and lower limit of a specific type of voice*. There is no fixed limit for individuals; many baritones have no trouble singing a top C, for example.

**Recitative:**  The bridge between arias* linked by spoken passages and through-composed opera. A way of singing the spoken section to the accompaniment of a harpsichord as a rule; most operas using extensive *recitatives* belong to the eighteenth century or earlier periods. Music is thus continuous, but sections are clearly subdivided between sung music and musically recited words. (See also 'Melodrama'.) The introduction to an aria is also known as 'recitative'.

**Records:**  Recordings of operas* or operatic arias* can be bought today in many forms, even including videotapes and videodiscs, which are no less than fully filmed operas. It must be remembered that anything other than recordings of live performances can be doctored to produce an article vastly better than anything even the best cast can offer in an opera house. Modern records should not be used as a standard of excellence; technology has as much to do with their quality as the performers. At the opposite end of the scale, old recordings should not be condemned if their performers are not perfect. In their day re-takes did not exist and a singer may have been out of form or even indisposed on the day of recording. A good singer is good if his *average* standard in many *live* performances is consistently high. He or she should not be judged through the medium of technical wizardry, which can make bad singers sound good and good singers sound bad. (See also 'Acoustic recordings' and 'Electric recordings.)

**Register:**  There are certain 'registers' in the voice in which a type of gear change occurs. It is the smoothing over of those changes which are the secret of good teaching and, ultimately, good singing. The register changes at a lower level for a baritone

125

HOW TO

ENJOY

OPERA

WITHOUT

REALLY

TRYING

than for a tenor. He therefore needs re-training if he wants to turn tenor, as many do. The fact that he already has the tenor range at the top is immaterial.

**Rehearsal:** The fact that extensive rehearsals are required for a limited number of performances in the case of operas is responsible for the high fees demanded by singers; they can make much more in a single concert than in six performances of operas and the weeks of rehearsals required. The day when singers arrived in a city and only met their fellow-artists during the actual performance in front of an audience have long passed, except in last minute emergencies. Rehearsals take far more time these days than performances and every cast change means new rehearsals by a very large number of people!

**Renaissance:** Once the term referred to a specific period in the history of art. Today it is used to describe anything existing which happens to come back into fashion, temporarily or permanently.

**Repertoire:** The works which appear in a season of opera or can be staged by an opera company at any one time. The range of works 'in the repertoire' of a singer are the operas or arias* or songs which he or she knows by heart. The 'repertoire' governs every opera season or concert, for its existence cuts down on rehearsals for artist and company alike.

**Repertory company:** An opera company which engages its artists and staff on an annual basis and produces operas for the major part of each year, in the northern hemisphere roughly from September to the following June. (See also 'Stagione' company.)

**Revival:** The normal description of an opera production which has been staged previously by the same company, but the term can be more loosely applied to any revival of an opera, particularly an obscure one. A 'new' production of an old favourite may hold surprises for an audience, while a 'revival'

126

means that they have seen it before, though probably with different singers.

**Rock opera:**    Quite a valid description, even though academics do not like to admit it. Any dramatic work with any kind of music is an opera. If its music can be described as 'rock-'n-roll', the result is a rock opera. Few, very few, have proved to be of lasting value up to now.

**Romantic music:**    Romantic operas in this context are not love stories, but belong to the 'romantic period', which is roughly the mid-nineteenth century. Musically its values are the kind of lush tunes which remain popular to this day, but its beginning or end are vague and its style can vary substantially. Verdi and Wagner make an unlikely pair, but both belonged to the romantic period. The dramatic content of romantic operas is equally varied; it is weighted very heavily toward extremes, the supernatural, genuine romance, historical spectacle, the grotesque, swash-buckling heroes and swooning heroines. Love and death (*Liebes-tod**) and mad scenes* predominate.

**Rubato:**    The art of varying the tempo* of the music slightly to enhance its dramatic impact.

**Saga:**    Literally, a Nordic legend, but more commonly, and sometimes sarcastically, used to describe the story of an opera.

**Satire:**    Making fun of something which is serious, usually in the form of a comic opera with political overtones, e.g. the works of Offenbach or Gilbert and Sullivan. Satirising opera itself used to be a common practice, but seldom occurs today. Now largely restricted to using familiar tunes from operas to accompany words which bear no relation to the music, the only first-class example of recent years was Franz Reizenstein's *Let's Fake an Opera*, written for television! (The Hoffnung Interplanetary Music Festival in 1958.)

HOW TO

ENJOY

OPERA

WITHOUT

REALLY

TRYING

***Scene:*** An act* of an opera which is too short to justify being followed by an interval. Scenes can vary in length and no rules exist as to their number or placement; you can have an opera in two acts and ten scenes (Mozart's *Magic Flute*), which has three scenes in the first act, but seven in the second!

***Scenery:*** The backgrounds and surroundings in which singers perform operas. Originally mostly painted back-cloths, modern realism and technology have enabled some truly astounding realistic sets* to be built. The design of scenery largely depends on the demands made by the dramatic narrative and the placements of intervals* or pauses during which scene-changes can take place. The size and shape of stages* also varies.

***Score:*** The musical notes of an opera as performed, written or printed.

***Serenade:*** A love song, preferably sung under the window of a lady. (The word has alternative musical meanings outside opera.)

***Set:*** The scenery for a particular act* or scene* of an opera. The most spectacular sets were created for French grand operas* in the nineteenth century. It can be said that opera reached its greatest popularity when the sets provided as great an attraction as the singers or the music, hence the abundance of natural disasters featured in grand operas. Earthquakes, floods, erupting volcanoes, avalanches, and the like, were abundant at a time when the general public had never seen films or television. The effects which helped to sell a Meyerbeer opera would be laughable today; in their time they amazed the public.

***Sextet:*** See 'Duet'.

***Sight lines:*** A most important part of the seating in theatres. Theoretically, the occupant of every seat should be able to see the whole stage. In practice, the rule is that they should be able to see the centre of the back wall of the stage. But very few opera houses do not have large numbers of seats from which you see a lot less than that. Modern opera houses are attempting to improve sight lines by raking the stalls* (orchestra*) steeply and adopting the European-style unbroken rows of seats without aisles. Balancing the advantage of seeing well against having to climb lots of stairs and clambering over other people to get to your seat is not easy.

**Singing teachers:**   The most important and most dangerous part of any singer's career is the choice of teacher(s). One who suits this voice may be disastrous for another and each convinces his or her pupil that he or she is the possessor of 'the' method which will make the student a star. Nobody, repeat: nobody, has ever found the secret of good singing. It varies from person to person and even the best natural voice can be ruined by a bad teacher, or a good teacher as well! Anyone born with a good voice requires one thing: intelligence. Unfortunately, the young are too easily influenced by strong personalities and an awful lot of teachers have an almost hypnotic hold on their pupils.

**Snobs:**   Equals opera-goers, say some. And with a degree of justification. Opera has always attracted the socially prominent, because it was once the exclusive property of the upper classes. The musical snob today is more sophisticated. He learns all the right words and intimidates others with his superior knowledge. Since the appreciation of an art is not a science, this results in the blind leading the blind. In enjoying opera ignorance can be bliss. Knowledge can add to your enjoyment, not lead to it.

**Soprano:**   The highest of the female voices. (See also 'Voice' and 'Top Notes'.)

**Sprechgesang:**   A German word meaning 'spoken song'. It is usually applied to modern '*recitative*'*. Some contemporary pieces of music theatre* contain nothing but *Sprechgesang*, which becomes monotonous very quickly, unless it is accompanied by extraordinary stage effects or interrupted by substantially different types of music, sung or instrumental.

**Stage:**   Used as a verb, it means to put an opera together and

129

HOW TO

ENJOY

OPERA

WITHOUT

REALLY

TRYING

can be done by either a producer/director* or an opera company. The 'stage' itself is the acting area visible to the audience. It should have extensive operational facilities in terms of lighting, lifts, a tower to accommodate scenery which is 'flown' upwards out of sight and many technical effects to assist the producer. From the singers' point of view, the stage can affect the projection of the voice into the auditorium. The variety of stages is endless and so is their shape in relation to sight lines*.

**Stagione companies:**   The type of opera company which carries only the administrative staff on a permanent basis and engages singers for limited seasons, usually paying everybody by the performance. The *stagione* company is becoming more and more popular. It has greater flexibility and its repertoire* is not restricted by contracted singers, who must be used to justify their continued employment. On the other hand, it is very hard to achieve consistent excellence with what can only be described as 'casual labour'. The fact is that some very major companies have done so.

**Stalls:**   The seating in the area on the ground floor of the auditorium* in front of the stage. Depending on the rake of the floor, the stalls* (also known as 'the orchestra'*) can be the best or the worst seats in the house. Side and back stalls should by rights be sold at a cheaper price, but very often are not.

**Subsidies:**   Another word for funding*.

**Suite:**   An orchestral pot-pourri of tunes from an opera, usually created by the composer himself. Most suites from operas are the best bits from works which have failed with the public on stage, though exceptions exist. Suites produce additional income for composers.

**Supernumerary:**   Another name for Extra*.

**Supratitles:**   Another name for Surtitles*.

**Surtitles:**   The most common name for the recent invention which projects translations on a screen above the stage when operas are performed in a foreign language, a live equivalent of the 'subtitles' used in films. Other names for the method, all coined for copyright reasons only, are Supratitles and SurCaps.

***Technique:*** The way of doing things. In the case of opera it is applied almost exclusively to the technique of singing, as opposed to the quality or size of a voice. A good 'technique' can make much of a small or unbeautiful voice, while world-beating star voices fail to make the grade because the singer cannot adapt to opera's particular demands. It is true to say that an opera singer's voice lies in the head, not the throat.

***Tempo:*** An Italian word used as 'speed' rather than the more correct translation 'time'. Conductors may set the speed, but if a singer decides to alter the *tempo*, he has little choice but to follow — during a performance. (What happens afterwards is another matter again.) Conventions* demand certain speeds which are contrary to the composer's intentions, many singers like to show the power of their lungs by holding on to a note as long as possible, others demonstrate the ability to run quickly and (we hope) accurately through coloratura*. Some types of music lend themselves readily to minor variations in speed, known as *rubato*. Everything depends on the overall agreement reached during rehearsals*. All parts of the whole must assume the same *tempo* or the result will be chaos.

***Tenor:*** The highest male voice. See 'Voice' and 'Top notes'.

***Text:*** See 'Libretto'.

***Tickets:*** See 'Box Office'.

***Tonal quality:*** The indefinable something which makes the human voice as distinctive as a finger print. A hundred tenors can sing the same note and all will sound different. Voice quality depends on the shape and size of both the vocal cords and the brains of a singer. Beautiful voices can be 'round', 'smooth', 'full',

HOW TO

ENJOY

OPERA

WITHOUT

REALLY

TRYING

'steady', 'warm' and much more — and those are only a selection of *good* attributes! Other matters influencing voice production are *'vibrato'*\*, *tremolo* and less frequently used technical terms, always expressed in Italian.

**Top notes:**   Once upon a time the ringing top note was almost all that mattered. As recently as the 1950s Giacomo Lauri-Volpi, already past sixty, was still bringing down the house with his Top Cs, though his singing was by then, to put it mildly, distressing at times. The high notes produced by tenors with full voice are a comparatively recent innovation, begun about 1840. Before that tenors sang high notes *falsetto*\*. Making a small artificial sound, tenors were at times asked to go as high as F above Top C, something few major singers attempt today, when only full-throated notes are acceptable. Sopranos, naturally, can go higher. The now unattainable tenor Top F is easier for lyric than dramatic sopranos and freak voices (like Mado Robin) have recorded notes as high as B flat above the Top C. She is said to have sung even the C above Top C, but I don't think she recorded it.

**Tremolo:**   See *'Vibrato'*.

**Trio:**   See 'Duet'.

**Trilogy:**   Three operas making up a full evening. Wagner called his *Ring des Nibelungen* cycle a *tetralogy*; three operas and a 'preliminary evening'. *Das Rheingold* being a full-length opera, that makes four operas described as three!

**Trittico:**   The most famous of the triple bills, Puccini's three one-acters which are staged in one evening, *Il tabarro*, *Suor Angelica* and *Gianni Schicchi*.

**Verismo:**   The so-called 'naturalistic' form of opera which started with Mascagni's *Cavalleria Rusticana* in 1890. *Verismo* operas are supposed to deal with everyday subjects in a realistic manner, as opposed to earlier operas which were usually concerned with noblemen and princesses, while their music allowed plenty of room for applause. The *verismo* style did away with the arias*. Most 'veristic' operas have very violent subjects. Their 'realism' is seldom realistic in the modern sense of the term.

**Vernacular:**   The language of the audience. The words of the original must fit the music better than any translation, yet composers have always wanted the words of their operas to be understood, i.e. translated. Today star singers will only learn their parts in the original language, which can be used anywhere in the world. Yet even the most operatic of countries, Germany and Italy, still sing most operas in the vernacular as well as in the original language. There is room for both, of course, but the novice should understand what is being sung, be it translated by the singers or the ever-spreading Surtitles*.

**Version:**   Many famous operas have alternative versions, most composed or arranged by the composer himself. Verdi re-wrote several of his works under new names. Rossini kept using bits and pieces from earlier operas in later ones and more recent 'authentic' versions are accepted as the standard ones. Which version, or edition, any opera company uses is determined by its musical director* or the conductor*.

**Vibrato:**   Italian: vibration. Since sound consists of vibrations, every voice has '*vibrato*' of some sort. Very little *vibrato* produces what is known as a 'white' voice, a bland characterless voice. A strong *vibrato* in the voice creates a lot of volume and, if nice and even, is considered the most desirable. The moment the vibrations go too far, the control of the voice becomes difficult and it can change into a *tremolo*, a wobble. The distinction between *vibrato* and *tremolo* is frequently not made correctly and many a singer of unsteady voice has been accused of having 'a *vibrato*', which is like saying that having a strong voice is a bad thing. *Vibrato* is good, *tremolo* is bad.

**Videotape:**   Or videodisc, the two present methods of recording both picture and sound together, as was previously done on film. The new method wins, because its low cost brings it within the

HOW TO

ENJOY

OPERA

WITHOUT

REALLY

TRYING

reach of any opera buff, while film* is expensive, fragile and difficult to project.

***Vocalist:*** A person who sings, but never an opera singer. Vocalists need microphones to amplify their voices. To call a full-blooded tenor or dramatic soprano 'a vocalist' is little short of insulting. At best (which is stylistically not very good) you can say that a singer 'vocalises' well and the French word '*vocalise*' is a wordless piece of singing which occasionally finds its way into an opera, usually sung by the chorus as background to the action.

***Voice:*** That which, some say, is the only thing which matters in an opera. No composer would agree with this sentiment, but the singing must be good to realise the creator's intent and each part must be sung by a voice suitable for its music. There are too many varieties of voice to list here, but the principal ones and their range are as follows: '**Soprano**': G to Top C — F, according to the type of rôle. '**Mezzo-soprano**': the same G to not such a high top, usually B flat, the accent being on the lower register. '**Contralto**': F to F with more weight to the voice than a mezzo-soprano has. '**Tenor**': Two octaves to High C. '**Baritone**': C to A flat with the accent on the middle range. '**Bass-Baritone**': A flat to F. '**Bass**': E or even D to F; a **basso profundo** may go down to low G, but such notes are rarer than Top Ds for tenors in opera. Ideally each singer should produce an even sound from his or her lowest to his or her highest note. What is known as 'chest voice'* is only condemned in women, who need this deep masculine sound if volume is to be obtained in the lower notes. The head voice* is similarly condemned in men. In both cases it is very difficult to make the transition from low to high notes without an audible gear change. The singers from the so-called 'Golden Age' used both chest and head voice, often without a break in registers, and many modern singers can do the same. Yet the same critics who want to condemn these sounds are the ones who are always claiming that the Golden Age should be the model for new young singers!

# Quick Check List*

*This* list should tell you at a glance whether any specific work is suitable for the person who has no previous knowledge of opera.

Five alternative evaluations of each work are made and a brief summary of the opera is given. To some, the familiar music may be of primary importance, to others whether a work is light or dramatic. Some like old music and some like modern. The reader will have to balance the various factors to determine his or her own final choice.

*Warning:* Modern producers are capable of extraordinary interpretations and/or distortions of the scenic and dramatic aspects of individual operas. A few succeed brilliantly, while others produce utter chaos. We cannot predict here what kind of production you may see, but it may reasonably be assumed that the music will be left untouched.

It may also be wise to inquire in advance whether operas are sung in English or the original language. If the latter, the use of 'Surtitles' (projected translations) will greatly assist the novice in appreciating the opera being staged.

* Works listed here are those most likely to be staged in opera houses today. This list is not intended to be *academically* beyond reproach. It is presented as a guide for new opera goers, to indicate whether or not they will find a particular opera entertaining.

HOW TO

ENJOY

OPERA

WITHOUT

REALLY

TRYING

IDENTIFICATION CODE

*1 Overall effect:*

☆☆☆ Very enjoyable

☆☆ Quite enjoyable

☆ May appeal

— Unlikely to appeal to beginners

*2 Familiarity of the music:*

●●● Many famous arias and tunes

●● Easily accessible, even if unfamiliar

● Acceptable

— Unacceptable to beginners

*3 Value as theatrical entertainment:*

△△△ Very good

△△ Good

△ Passable

— Likely to bore beginners

*4 Subject matter:*

F Funny or very light

R Romantic love story

D Dramatic action

*5 Period of music:*

E Early or baroque music

M Mozart or similar style

N Nineteenth century romantic

T Twentieth century romantic

A Avant garde, modern

*Language:* The final entry under each opera is the language in which it is most likely to be heard if it is not played in the vernacular (the language of the audience); it is not necessarily the language in which it was written. The principal languages are abbreviated:

Eng. English    Fr. French    Ger. German    It. Italian

## LIST OF OPERAS

**Abduction from the Seraglio, The:** See *Entführung aus dem Serail.*

☆☆☆   ●●●   △△    *D  N*

**Aida** (Verdi) Grand spectacle of ancient Egypt. The slave Aida, daughter of King Amonasro of Ethiopia, loves the Egyptian army leader Radames, who is loved by Amneris, the Pharaoh's daughter. Radames is tricked into betraying the Egyptians and is buried alive with Aida. It. (See also Page 67)

☆       ●       △△    F   A

**Albert Herring** (Britten) An English village crowns innocent Albert 'May King', but the demon rum ruins Albert in the best and funniest possible way. Eng.

☆       ●       △      D   E

**Alceste** (Gluck) Greek mythology. Alceste offers herself as a human sacrifice to save her husband, but Hercules prevents her entry into Hades. Happy end! Fr.

☆       ●       △      D   E

**Alcina** (Handel) Complicated story of the sorceress Alcina who turns people into beasts on a magic island. It.

☆☆      ●       △△    D   T

**Amahl and the Night Visitors** (Menotti) Short Christmas story about a crippled boy and the Magi on the way to Bethlehem. Eng.

137

HOW TO

ENJOY

OPERA

WITHOUT

REALLY

TRYING

☆☆ ●● △△△ R N

**Andrea Chénier** (Giordano) Very full-blooded opera about the French revolution, with some sweeping music for big voices. Typical triangle, very similar to *Tosca*, with lovers going to guillotine together. It.

☆☆ ●● △△ D N

**Anna Bolena** (Donizetti) Part of a trilogy about English queens, the story of Anne Boleyn and Henry VIII. *Bel canto* opera with lots of fine singing. It.

☆ ● △△ F T

**Arabella** (Richard Strauss) A father with two daughters has only enough for one dowry and brings one girl up as a boy. Typical operetta plot, but highly literate and with fine music. Ger.

☆ ●● △ F T

**Ariadne auf Naxos** (Richard Strauss) Not much action, but nice music. A private performance of an opera is rehearsed and then performed. Ger.

☆☆ ●● △△ D N

**Attila** (Verdi) Typical rousing early Verdi music with strong dramatic action about the famous Hun and the people who try to kill him. It.

**Aufstieg und Fall der Stadt Mahagonny:** See *Rise and Fall of the City of Mahagonny*.

☆☆ ●● △△ D N

**Ballo in maschera, Un** (Verdi) (*A Masked Ball*) Later Verdi with a number of famous arias. The story of the assassination of Gustav III of Sweden. It.

**Barber of Seville, The:** See *Barbiere di Siviglia*

☆☆☆ ●●● △△△ C B

**Barbiere di Siviglia, Il** (Rossini) (*The Barber of Seville*) Ideal tuneful comedy opera. It. (See also Page 22)

☆☆☆  ●●  △△△  C  N

**Bartered Bride, The** (Smetana) Czech folk comedy with excellent plot about a shifty village marriage broker and the way the hero gets his girl *and* the money. Tuneful. Eng.

☆☆☆  ●●●  △△△  F  N

**Ba-ta-clan** (Offenbach) Satirical *chinoiserie*, an earlier French *Mikado*.

☆  ●●  △  F  N

**Beatrice and Benedict** (Berlioz) Based on Shakespeare's *Much Ado About Nothing*. Has one truly glorious long duet and some pleasant music. Fr.

☆☆☆  ●●●  △△△  F  N

**Belle Hélène, La** (Offenbach) Musically the best of all the Offenbach works, with uproarious comedy about Greek Gods. Ideal entertainment. Fr.

☆  ●  △  D  N

**Benvenuto Cellini** (Berlioz) Rarely performed very grand opera about the great Italian artist and the building of a statue. If staged at all, likely to be spectacular. Fr.

☆☆☆  ●●●  △△△  R  N

**Bohème, La** (Puccini) More famous tunes than any other opera. Fool-proof romantic plot about consumptive heroine and artists on the Left Bank of Paris. Ideal. It.

☆  ●●  △△  D  N

**Boris Godounov** (Mussorgsky) Slow-moving historical pageant of the Russian Tsar and the false pretender Dimitri. With great actor in central rôle can be very effective. Russian.

**Breasts of Tiresias, The:** See *Mamelles de Tirésias, Les*

☆☆☆  ●●  △△△  F  T

**Candide** (Bernstein) Unfamiliar modern musical gaining popularity. Eng. (See also Page 40)

139

HOW TO

ENJOY

OPERA

WITHOUT

REALLY

TRYING

☆　　●　　△　　C T

**Capriccio** (Richard Strauss) Slight comedy about a composer and poet arguing about which comes first, words or music. Ger.

☆　　●●　　△　　D N

**Capuleti e i Montecchi, I** (Bellini) Setting of Shakespeare's *Romeo and Juliet*. Pleasant music, but has a female Romeo and is not very exciting. It.

☆☆☆　●●●　△△△　D N

**Carmen** (Bizet) The most popular opera around. Bull-fighters and sex. Fr. (See also Page 53)

☆☆☆　●●●　△△△　D N

**Cavalleria Rusticana** (Mascagni) Italian peasants and jealousy. Very tuneful. It. (See also Page 49)

☆☆☆　●●　△△△　F N

**Cenerentola, La** (Rossini) The story of Cinderella with delightful music and some very funny twists to the plot. Recommended. It.

☆　　●　　△　　D M

**Clemenza di Tito, La** (Mozart) Least popular Mozart and heavy going, though the music is nice. The story of Emperor Titus of Rome and his marital problems. It.

☆☆☆　●●　△△　C B

**Comte Ory, Le** (Rossini) Very funny French farce with delightful music. What went on during the crusades. Contains everything but a chastity belt. Fr.

☆☆　●　△△△　D A

**Consul, The** (Menotti) Stark drama about political refugees. Very good theatre, but not much singing apart from one great aria. Eng.

☆☆☆ ●●● △△△ D N

**Contes d'Hoffman, Les** (Offenbach) (*The Tales of Hoffman*) Really four operas in one, comedy, drama, horror and more, featuring the romantic adventures of Hoffmann. Very tuneful and suitable for imaginative production. Fr.

**Coronation of Poppea, The:** See *Incoronazione di Poppea, L'*

☆☆ ●● △△ F M

**Così fan tutte** (Mozart) Slight comedy about a bet that women are fickle. Delightful music, but not a great deal of action. it.

☆☆ ●●● △△ F T

**Count of Luxembourg, The** (Lehár) The music keeps alive this somewhat dated operetta about a marriage in which the partners never see each other. Ger.

☆☆☆ ●●● △△ F T

**Countess Maritza** (Kálmán) The best operetta from the pen of Lehár's only serious competitor. Hungarian gypsy story with typical mixed identity plot. Ger.

☆ ● △ D T

**Cunning Little Vixen, The** (Janáček) Modern parable on human behaviour with all the characters as forest animals. Can be magical in good production, but very hard to stage well. Czech.

☆ ● △ D A

**Death in Venice** (Britten) Slow-moving plot of old man infatuated with (non-singing) boy in Venice. Not recommended for beginners. Eng.

☆☆ ● △△ D T

**Dialogues des Carmélites** (Poulenc) Surprisingly tuneful tale of order of nuns which is wiped out during French revolution. Fr.

HOW TO

ENJOY

OPERA

WITHOUT

REALLY

TRYING

☆　●●　△　　D　E

**Dido and Aeneas** (Purcell) Story of Queen Dido of Carthage, who kills herself when Aeneas is ordered to go to Italy. Very tuneful, but only for lovers of early music. Eng.

☆　●●　△　　D　N

**Don Carlos** (Verdi) The most forbidding score from Verdi, though it contains some superb music and many known arias. The battle between Philip II of Spain and his son Carlos, who loves his father's young wife. Very dark and gloomy. It.

☆☆☆　●●●　△△　　D　M

**Don Giovanni** (Mozart) contains much of Mozart's best music, to re-enact the adventures of the original Don Juan and his ultimate descent to hell. Too many scenes, but great opportunities for good singing and acting. Some comedy as well as stark drama. It.

☆☆☆　●●●　△△△　F　N

**Don Pasquale** (Donizetti) An almost fool-proof comic masterpiece with excellent music. How the elderly Pasquale is tricked into letting his nephew marry the girl of his choice. Less complex than *The Barber of Seville*, but just as enjoyable. It.

☆☆　●　△　　D　N

**Don Quichotte** (Massenet) Faithful re-telling of Cervantes' *Don Quixote*, but requires great actor for the lead. Fr.

—　　—　　—　　D　A

**Donnerstag aus Licht** (Stockhausen) Modern multi-media work. Hardly an opera, though played in opera houses. Way out.

☆☆☆　●●　△△　　F　A

**Dreigroschenoper, Die** (Weill) (*The Threepenny Opera*) A modernistic 'operetta', the first political satire written during the 1920s depression in Germany. Much copied and updated because of the unique style of Weill's music and Bertold Brecht's brilliant text. Hit song: 'Mack, the Knife'. Ger.

— — — D A

**Duke Bluebeard's Castle** (Bartók) Symbolic and heavy drama of Bluebeard and his wives. Only for Bartók fans, but very short. Hungarian.

QUICK CHECK LIST

☆ ● — D N

**Edgardo** (Puccini) Early Puccini; his only failure. Not in any way typical Puccini. Only ever staged as a curiosity. It.

— — △ D T

**Elektra** (Richard Strauss) Heavy Greek mythology. Very loud, very fine music, but must be superbly sung and acted to have any effect at all. Ger.

☆☆☆ ●●● △△△ F N

**Elisir d'amore, L'** (Donizetti) (*The Elixir of Love*) Delightful rustic comedy with plenty of really good tunes and some very funny situations. One of the most famous of all tenor arias: 'Down her cheek a pearly tear'. It.

☆ ●● △ F M

**Entführung aus dem Serail, Die** (Mozart) (*The Abduction from the Seraglio* or simply *The Seraglio*) Primitive comedy with spoken dialogue which survives solely on basis of some fine Mozart arias and, in good productions, a fine central figure of fun, the eunuch Osmin. Ger.

☆☆ ●● △△ D N

**Ernani** (Verdi) Very old-fashioned and at times ludicrous plot about chivalry, but full of superb tunes and lots of action. It.

☆ ●● △ R N

**Eugene Onegin** (Tchaikovsky) Poet rejects young girl, then wants her when she has married another. Sob story without much action, but pleasant music. Russian.

— — △ D E

**Fairy Queen, The** (Purcell) Ye olde English playe based on

143

HOW TO

ENJOY

OPERA

WITHOUT

REALLY

TRYING

*A Midsummer-Night's Dream*. Often revived, but only as an historical curio. Eng.

☆　●　△△　F　N

**Falstaff** (Verdi) A major masterpiece, but very unlike other Verdi operas. With first-class producer can be quickly enjoyed. In poor hands: stay away. It.

☆　●●　△△　D　N

**Fanciulla del West, La** (Puccini) (*The Girl of the Golden West*) The only genuine 'horse opera', set in the Californian Gold Rush. Silent-film-corny story but plenty of action with some very pleasant music. It.

☆☆☆　●●●　△△　R　N

**Faust** (Gounod) Famous tale of man who sold his soul to the devil. Very tuneful. Once the world's most popular opera, now considered a bit 'soppy', but full of action and special effects. Fr. (See also Page 71)

☆　●●　△△　D　N

**Fidelio** (Beethoven) Uneven, only opera written by Beethoven. Good dramatic action with spoken dialogue. Prefer in English initially. Famous tribute to human liberty. Ger.

☆☆☆　●●　△△　F　N

**Fille du Régiment, La** (Donizetti) (*The Daughter of the Regiment* or, in Italian: *La figlia del reggimento*) Military lass brought up by a regiment of soldiers turns out to be duchess' lost child. Delightful music and funny situations. Fr.

☆☆☆　●●●　△△△　F　N

**Fledermaus, Die** (Johann Strauss) (*The Bat*) Foolproof operetta-turned-opera. Go and see it. Ger.

☆　●●　△　R　N

**Fliegende Holländer, Der** (Wagner) (*The Flying Dutchman*) Gloomy and static early Wagner opera with some fine familiar music. Ger.

**Flying Dutchman, The:** See *Fliegende Holländer, Der*

**Force of Destiny, The:** See *Forza del destino, La*

☆☆  ●●●  △△  D  N

**Forza del destino, La** (Verdi) (*The Force of Destiny*) Exciting blood-and-thunder nineteenth century action drama with excellent music, but complicated plot of brother following his sister's lover to kill him in revenge for — who cares? Very long, but very tuneful. It.

☆☆  ●●  △△  F  N

**Fra Diavolo** (Auber) Operetta-cum-opera with funny plot about a robbing hood and his ludicrous victims. Once subject of Laurel and Hardy film. Need I say more? Fr.

☆  ●  —  R  T

**Francesca da Rimini** (Zandonai) Recently becoming popular again after years of neglect. Typical heavy love drama of star-crossed lovers. It.

☆  —  —  R  T

**Frau ohne Schatten, Die** (Richard Strauss) (*The Woman Without a Shadow*) A monumental work of magic and mysticism which can be quite overwhelming, but not for beginners. Very long. Ger.

☆  ●  △△△  F  N

**Gianni Schicchi** (Puccini) Last of three short operas making *Il trittico*. Very funny and brilliant music, but only one famous tune: 'Oh, my beloved father'. Should be heard first in English. It.

☆☆  ●●  △△  D  N

**Gioconda, La** (Ponchielli) Impossibly complex Italian 'grand' opera with sweeping tunes, burning ships, blind mothers and self-sacrificing lovers. Needs great singers and contains the famous 'Dance of the Hours'. Rarely performed now, more's the pity. It.

HOW TO

ENJOY

OPERA

WITHOUT

REALLY

TRYING

**Girl of the Golden West, The:** See *Fanciulla del West, La*

☆     —     —     D   E

**Giulio Cesare** (Handel) (*Julius Caesar*) Probably the most famous of Handel's umpteen operas. Like most of the others, little more than a static series of arias sung one after the other. No action at all. Only for Handel addicts. It.

☆     ●     —     D   N

**Götterdämmerung, Die** (Wagner) (*The Twilight of the Gods*) The last, and longest of the four operas which make up *The Ring of the Nibelungen*, Wagner's guarantee of immortality. Some superb and very loud music, but at six hours too much for any but devoted Wagnerites. Ger.

—     —     △△     D   A

**Grand Macabre, Le** (Ligeti) Fantastic, grotesque and erotic modern theatre piece. Difficult singing and difficult music. Hungarian.

☆     ●     △     D   N

**Guillaume Tell** (Rossini) (*William Tell*) Rossini's last opera and his only 'grand' opera. Totally unlike his other works. Very good for opera-lovers, but too cumbersome for you. Fr.

☆☆     ●●     △△     F   N

**Hänsel und Gretel** (Humperdinck) (*Hansel and Gretel*) Intended as an opera for children, as the story remains; the opera's music has made it immortal. Its Wagnerian size and un-Wagnerian tunefulness make it an unlikely, but most suitable introduction to the methods and principles of Humperdinck's mentor: Richard Wagner. Ger.

☆☆     ●     △△     D   T

**Help, Help, the Globolinks!** (Menotti) Children's opera with appeal for adults. Invaders from outer space beaten by music!

—     —     —     D   E

**Incoronazione di Poppea, L'** (Monteverdi) (*The Coronation of*

*Poppea*) Very early music. Complex story (non-factual) how Nero came to marry Poppea. Only for baroque fans. It.

☆ — △ F T

**Intermezzo** (Richard Strauss) Private joke based on Strauss' strange marriage to an impossible wife. Only for Strauss fans. Ger.

☆ — — D E

**Iphigénie en Aulide** and **Iphigénie en Tauride** (Gluck) Two long operas on Greek mythology of great value historically, being among first to link musical content with words. Fr.

☆ ●● △ D N

**Isabeau** (Mascagni) Incredible, but true: an opera about the Lady Godiva legend with some very fine music, but an impossible plot to stage convincingly. It.

☆☆☆ ●● △△△ F N

**Italiana in Algeri, L'** (Rossini) *(The Italian Girl in Algiers)* Delightful comedy about a girl captured by Arab ruler and intended for his harem. Highly recommended. It.

☆ ●● △△ D N

**Jenůfa** (Janáček) Highly dramatic Czech opera without obvious tunes, but very tuneful music. Very emotional and moving when well produced and sung. Czech.

☆ ● △ D N

**Juive, La** (Halévy) *(The Jewess)* Very grand French opera, bloodthirsty plot about Jews and the Inquisition. One famous aria and a lot of action. Fr.

— — △△ C A

**Junge Lord, Der** (Henze) *(The Young Lord)* Very funny plot about man who tries to pass off a monkey as a foreign aristocrat. Fine

147

HOW TO

ENJOY

OPERA

WITHOUT

REALLY

TRYING

play with incidental music. Unlikely to appeal on musical grounds. Ger.

—    —    △    D   A

**Káťa Kabanová** (Janáček) Grim family drama. No tunes. Czech.

☆    ●    △    D   N

**Khovantchina** (Mussorgsky) Historical political plot. Pleasant but unmemorable music. Not for beginners. Russian.

—    —    —    D   A

**King Priam** (Tippett) Greek mythology with modern music. Eng.

☆    ●    △△   F   A

**Kluge, Die** (Orff) (*The Wise Woman*) German fairy tale using catchy, but unusual music. Can be very enjoyable if sung in language of audience. Ger.

—    —    —    D   A

**Knot Garden, The** (Tippett) Modern plot about marital infidelity and homosexuality. Eng.

—    —    —    D   A

**Lady Macbeth of Mtsensk** (Shostakovitch) Very gloomy sexual plot set in Russian backwoods and ending in several murders. Russian.

☆☆    ●●    △△   F   A

**Let's Make an Opera** (Britten) Literally: make your own opera, a children's opera with audience participation. Enjoyable for adults as well. Eng.

☆    ●    △    D   N

**Life for the Tsar, A** (Glinka) The opera which started Russian nationalistic opera, but is less heavy than the later, more famous works. Needs good spectacle, but not really for newcomers. Russian.

**Lohengrin** (Wagner) The only Wagner opera which is readily accessible. A little long, but some famous tunes including the 'original' Wedding March ('Here Comes the Bride'). Setting: when knighthood was in flower. Ger.

☆☆　●●　△　D　N

**Lombardi, I** (Full title: *I Lombardi alla prima crociata*) (Verdi) (*The Lombards at the First Crusade*) Knights and infidels battling for the Holy Land, with two brothers battling on the side lines for one girl. Rousing tunes. It.

☆　　●　　—　　D　T

**Louise** (Charpentier) Modern working-class subject. Unusual and would appeal to anyone who loves Paris. Fr.

—　　—　　△　　F　A

**Love of Three Oranges, The** (Prokofiev) Strange modern love story, mixture of Russian fairy tales and abstract avant-garde ideas from the 1920s. Eng.

☆☆　●●●　△△　R　N

**Lucia di Lammermoor** (Donizetti) The opera which made mad scenes famous. A great vehicle for a great star and some famous music, but on the slow side. It.

☆　　●●　△△　D　N

**Lucrezia Borgia** (Donizetti) Strange story twists about the famous poisoner of history. Can be spectacular with fine singers and good production. It.

☆　　●●　△　D　N

**Luisa Miller** (Verdi) Some great Verdi tunes in the usual complicated story which does not make much sense. Very much a connoisseur's piece. It.

☆　　—　△△　D　A

**Lulu** (Berg) Good old-fashioned decadence with murders,

149

HOW TO

ENJOY

OPERA

WITHOUT

REALLY

TRYING

seductions. Ideal subject for a soft-porn film, but very way-out music. Needs great actors rather than singers. Ger.

**Lustigen Weiber von Windsor, Die:** See *Merry Wives of Windsor, The*

**Lustige Witwe, Die:** See *Merry Widow, The*.

☆☆   ●●   △     D  N

**Macbeth** (Verdi) Shakespeare's famous play made a bit too tuneful by young Verdi. True to original, but on the gloomy side — naturally! It.

☆☆   ●●●   △△   R  N

**Madam Butterfly** (Puccini) One of the most famous of all operas about mixed 'marriage' between American sailor and Japanese geisha. Decidedly soppy-romantic, but with glorious music. It.

—     —    △     D  A

**Makropoulos Affair, The** (Janáček) Good macabre story about 300-year-old woman and her way of rejuvenating herself. Vehicle for a fine actress with good voice and interesting subject, if sung in your language. Czech.

☆☆   ●    △△△  F  A

**Mamelles de Tirésias, Les** (Poulenc) (*The Breasts of Tiresias*) Completely crazy, but very funny short opera with cabaret-style music and dressing (or undressing) which is as important as the music. The leading man gives birth to 40,000 babies! It's foolish, but it's fun — if it is sung in your language. Fr.

☆☆☆   ●●   △△   R  N

**Manon** (Massenet) should not be mistaken for the next work. One of the great love stories of history based on sexual versus financial attractions. Should Manon live for love or money. Love kills her, of course. Beautiful music and golden opportunities for the right leading couple. Fr.

☆☆☆  ●●●  △△  R  N
**Manon Lescaut** (Puccini) The same story as the previous, but treated as full-blooded Italian drama with plenty of loud bawling which, when well-executed, can be very exciting. It.

☆☆  ●●  △  D  N
**Maria Stuarda** (Donizetti) (*Mary Stuart*) Completely false history, but fine *bel canto* style treatment of the fight between Elizabeth and Mary over the British throne and a supposed lover. It.

☆☆  ●●  △△  R  N
**Martha** (Flotow) was once one of the most popular of operas and has some famous tunes, but is now an old-fashioned love story rather than the once funny comedy it used to be. Ger.

**Mastersingers of Nuremberg, The:** See *Meistersinger von Nürnberg, Die*

☆☆  ●●  △△  F  N
**Matrimonio Segreto, Il** (Cimarosa) (*The Secret Marriage*) Typical 'love-will-find-a-way' farce with delightful music. It.

☆  ●  —  D  N
**Médée** (Cherubini) (*Medea*) Often revived for great personalities like Callas. Without such a lead, just an old-fashioned singing vehicle. Fr.

☆☆☆  ●  △△△  D  A
**Medium, The** (Menotti) A superb piece of dramatic theatre needing very little staging beyond brilliant performances by an old woman, the Medium, a young girl and a dumb boy. Had long run on Broadway in 1946 before world-wide success. Almost operatic Hitchcock. Eng.

☆  ●●  △  D  N
**Mefistofele** (Boito) (*Mephistopheles*) An alternative to Gounod's Faust based on the same original, but totally different. Some great music, but lacks continuity and the divine spark, though

151

HOW TO

ENJOY

OPERA

WITHOUT

REALLY

TRYING

much of the music is vastly better than Gounod's famous masterpiece. It.

☆☆　●　△△　R　N

**Meistersinger von Nürnberg, Die** (Wagner) (*The Mastersingers of Nuremberg*) Wagner's only real comedy, but even that is so long that the chuckles are eclipsed by the admittedly great music. At least it has a happy end, but it is not an opera to start with. Ger.

☆☆☆　●●●　△△△　F　N

**Merry Widow, The** (Lehár) The world's most famous operetta, which has by now surely been in the repertoire of every opera company. Good music, a plausible plot, a little comedy — success! Ger.

☆☆　●●　△△　F　N

**Merry Wives of Windsor, The** (Nicolai) A lighter alternative to Verdi's *Falstaff*, both based on the same Shakespeare text. Very tuneful and funny and more suitable for newcomers to opera than Verdi's much better opera. Ger.

—　　—　　—　　D　A

**Midsummer Marriage, The** (Tippett) An abstract modern myth which even experienced audiences find hard to understand and Tippett's music is an acquired taste. Eng.

☆　　●　　△　F　A

**Midsummer-Night's Dream, A** (Britten) Modern, but so cleverly written that the old play can be made most entertaining, if really well produced. The author, one William Shakespeare, sees to that. Eng.

☆　　●●　△　D　N

**Mignon** (Thomas) Many very famous arias, but the opera itself is old-fashioned and 'grand' in the French manner. Rarely revived, but has a lot of very nice music in it. Fr.

152

☆　　●●　　△　　D　N

**Mosè in Egitto** (Rossini) (*Moses in Egypt*) One of Rossini's serious operas with one tremendous prayer and a lot of singing, but nothing memorable. It.

—　　—　　△　　D　A

**Moses und Aron** (Schoenberg) (*Moses and Aron*) The biblical text told in very modern musical speech. Only successful when featuring a great, big juicy orgy. Ger.

—　　—　　—　　D　N

**Mozart and Salieri** (Rimsky-Korsakov) Russian opera long forgotten but for the title and now met with renewed interest since the film *Amadeus*. Even now, revivals are rare, and deserve to be. Russian.

☆☆☆　●●　　△△△　D　N

**Nabucco** (Verdi) Verdi's first success because of rousing tunes and exciting drama in spite of biblical subject. It.

☆☆☆　●●●　△△△　F　N

**Nacht in Venedig, Eine** (J. Strauss) (*A Night in Venice*) Most tuneful Viennese operetta. Ger.

**Night in Venice:** See *Nacht in Venedig*

☆☆　　●●●　△△　D　N

**Norma** (Bellini) The *Hamlet* for sopranos. Needs great star. Fine music and tuneful, but slow story about Druid priestesses. It.

☆　　—　　△△　F　A

**Nose, The** (Shostakovitch) Surrealist romp. In hands of brilliant producer has been a big success, but very difficult to make it work. How do you play a nose? Russian.

☆☆☆　●●●　△△△　F　M

**Nozze di Figaro, Le** (Mozart) (*The Marriage of Figaro*) Ideal comedy, delightful music, but must be seen first in English. It. (See also Page 23)

HOW TO

ENJOY

OPERA

WITHOUT

REALLY

TRYING

—    —    —    D   E

**Orfeo** (Monteverdi) (*Orpheus*) Not to be mistaken for Gluck's *Orfeo ed Euridice*. Very esoteric. Not for beginners. It.

☆    ●●    △    D   E

**Orfeo ed Euridice** (Gluck) (*Orpheus and Euridice*) A milestone in opera history and very pleasant music, but slow for a beginner, unless he has an interest in it. It.

**Orpheus and Euridice:** See *Orfeo ed Euridice*

☆☆☆    ●●●    △△△    F   N

**Orpheus in the Underworld** (Offenbach) Delightful send-up of the many Orpheus operas about a husband rescuing his wife from Hell. One of the best comic operas ever written. Fr.

☆☆    ●●    △△    D   N

**Otello** (Verdi) Shakespeare's *Othello* set to music. Possibly the best opera ever written, if not the most popular. Tuneful, dramatic and, if well sung, a great experience, but perhaps on the heavy side for a start. It.

☆☆☆    ●●●    △△△    D   N

**Pagliacci** (Leoncavallo) (*Clowns*) Perfect introduction to dramatic opera. Full of famous arias and a very exciting story of love and jealousy. It. (See also Page 49)

—    ●    —    D   N

**Parsifal** (Wagner) Pseudo-religious drama of very great length. Only for Wagnerians. Ger.

☆☆    ●●●    △    D   N

**Pearlfishers, The** (Bizet) Early Bizet with some famous tunes and, usually, very pretty scenery. Dull story, but worth a try. Fr.

☆    ●    —    D   T

**Pelléas and Melisande** (Debussy) Very attractive music with hardly any plot, but slow and not for beginners. Fr.

☆☆    ●●    △△△    F    N

**Périchole, La** (Offenbach) Slightly more romantic than funny Offenbach. Enjoyable. Fr.

☆    —    △    D    A

**Peter Grimes** (Britten) Most popular of modern operas about a misfit in an English fishing village. Not for starters. Eng.

☆☆    ●●●    △△△    D    T

**Porgy and Bess** (Gershwin) Gershwin's only opera, a Broadway musical with pretensions. Clever lyrics, strong drama and some famous tunes. Eng. (See also Page 36)

☆☆    ●●    △△    D    N

**Puritani, I** (Bellini) (*The Puritans*) Typical nonsensical story saved by some superb music, but needs outstanding soprano and tenor. Lots of high notes and three (!) Mad Scenes. It.

☆    ●    △△    D    A

**Rake's Progress, The** (Stravinsky) Famous story based on Hogarth. Can be very good, but risky for beginners. Eng.

—    —    —    D    A

**Rape of Lucretia, The** (Britten) Modern re-telling of old story. Only for Britten fans. Eng.

☆    ●    —    D    N

**Rienzi** (Wagner) Early Wagner. Long and heavy, but music has some catchy Italian-style tunes. Ger.

☆☆☆    ●●●    △△△    D    N

**Rigoletto** (Verdi) The first and still best example of what has made opera popular today. Good tunes, lots of action and drama and can even pass with inferior singers. Often performed now in modern dress. Recommended highly. It. (See also Page 50)

☆    ●    —    D    N

**Ring des Nibelungen, Der** (Wagner) (*The Ring of the Nibelungen*) Series of four operas performed in sequence. An opera

HOW TO

ENJOY

OPERA

WITHOUT

REALLY

TRYING

marathon. Not recommended to start, though considered the ultimate masterpiece by many. Ger.

☆☆　　●　　△△　　D　T
**Rise and Fall of the City of Mahagonny, The** (Weill) Modern political parable which can be very entertaining and has some genuine pop tunes in the score. Ger.

☆☆　　●●　　△△　　D　N
**Romeo and Juliet** (Gounod) Faithful reconstruction of Shakespeare set to music. Very pleasant, but nothing special. Fr.

☆☆　　●●　　△△　　D　N
**Rondine, La** (Puccini) (*The Dove*) One of the least known of Puccini's works, very light and much under-estimated. A very pleasant evening if well performed. It.

☆☆　　●●　　△△　　F　T
**Rosenkavalier, Der** (R. Strauss) (*The Cavalier of the Rose*) Richard Strauss' most famous work has much comedy and fine music, but is on the long side. Leave for later. Ger.

☆☆　　●●　　△△　　D　N
**Rusalka** (Dvořak) Very beautiful fairy tale about water nymph who falls for a mortal. Lovely music and not too long. Czech.

☆　　●●　　△　　D　N
**Sadko** (Rimsky-Korsakov) Russian fairy tale. Very long, very spectacular if staged in large theatre, but not very appealing to Western audiences. Russian.

☆　　●　　△△　　D　T
**Salome** (R. Strauss) Scandalous Oscar Wilde plot. Very 'decadent' and with famous 'Dance of the Seven Veils'. Very exciting finish, but only for connoisseurs. Ger.

☆☆　　●●　　△△　　D　N
**Samson and Delilah** (Saint-Saëns) Famous story with some very

156

fine arias and ensembles, but not exactly 'popular' except as vehicle for famous singers. Fr.

☆☆   ●●   △△   F   M
**Schauspieldirektor, Der** (Mozart) (*The Impresario*) Not really an opera, but a short play about competing prima donnas with Mozart music. Ger.

☆☆   ●●   △△   F   N
**Secret of Susanna, The** (Wolf-Ferrari) Short opera. Enjoyable romp about a heroine who smokes! It.

☆   ●●   —   D   N
**Semiramide** (Rossini) A great vehicle for a great soprano, some fine tunes, but a total mess as an opera. It.

☆   ●●   △   F   M
**Serva padrona, La** (Pergolesi) (*The Mistress as Maid*) Popular early one-acter. Pleasant, but unmemorable. It.

☆☆   ●●   △△   D   N
**Simon Boccanegra** (Verdi) Very good, but lesser Verdi. Dramatic story of Venetian politics with slow patches, but good highlights. Leave until later. It.

☆☆   ●●   △△   F   N
**Sonnambula, La** (Bellini) (*The Sleepwalker*) Very tuneful pastoral comedy with sad overtones which, if well sung, can be very appealing. It.

☆☆   ●●   △   D   N
**Suor Angelica** (Puccini) (*Sister Angelica*) Middle opera of the three which make up the *Trittico*. Very lovely, but inclined to monotony with an all-female cast and no action. It.

☆☆   ●●   △△   D   N
**Tabarro, Il** (Puccini) (*The Cloak*) First of the *Trittico* operas. Highly dramatic with good atmosphere and solid stretches of really fine music. Recommended. It.

HOW TO

ENJOY

OPERA

WITHOUT

REALLY

TRYING

**Tales of Hoffmann:** See *Contes d'Hoffmann, Les*

☆☆   ●●●   △△   D  N

**Tannhäuser** (Wagner) Wagner when tuneful can be very good even for a beginner. Though on the long side, has some very fine pages, but drags occasionally. Ger.

☆   ●●   △   D  N

**Thaïs** (Massenet) Sloppy mixture of religion versus sensuality with some nice music. Can be good with convincing leads. Fr.

**Threepenny Opera, The:** See *Dreigroschenoper, Die*

☆☆☆   ●●●   △△△   D  N

**Tosca** (Puccini) Another fool-proof starter. High drama and superb music. Yes! It. (See also Page 57)

☆   ●●   △   D  N

**Tristan and Isolde** (Wagner) Superb and rightly famous music, but a thirty-minute love duet? Much too long to start with. Ger.

☆☆☆   ●●●   △△△   D  N

**Trovatore, Il** (Verdi) A very exciting, but too complex plot. More recognisable music, arias, etc. than any other opera. Very highly recommended — with good singers! It. (See also Page 55)

☆   ●   △   D  N

**Troyens, Les** (Berlioz) (*The Trojans*) A French opera of Wagnerian length and good music, but only for connoisseurs. Fr.

☆☆   ●●●   △△△   D  N

**Turandot** (Puccini) Puccini's last opera. Not as easily accepted as earlier masterpieces, but with famous arias and great spectacular effects. It. (See also Page 69)

☆☆　●●　△△　D　N
**Turco in Italia, Il** (Rossini) (*The Turk in Italy*) Very funny and very tuneful. It.

—　　—　　△　　D　A
**Turn of the Screw, The** (Britten) Famous ghost story. Can be good theatre, but you can't whistle the tunes. Eng.

☆☆　●●●　△△　D　N
**Vêpres Siciliennes, Les** (Verdi) (*The Sicilian Vespers*) A French grand opera by Verdi with all the faults of grand opera, lots of complicated action, some fine tunes, but not for beginners. Fr. (Also played in Italian as *I vespri siciliani*)

☆☆☆　●●　△△　F　N
**Viva la Mamma** (Donizetti) Modern assembly of unknown Donizetti music. Tuneful and funny.

☆　　●　　△　　D　T
**War and Peace** (Prokofiev) Russian epic opera which can be surprisingly entertaining. Needs big production. Not for starters, though. Russian.

☆　　●●　△　　D　N
**Werther** (Massenet) Depressing subject with little action, but some nice music. Fr.

—　　—　　△　　D　A
**Wozzeck** (Berg) Famous modern opera, but a depressing story of a human misfit. Very modern music. Unlikely to appeal to the reader of this. Ger.

**Young Lord, The:** See *Junge Lord, Der*

HOW TO

ENJOY

OPERA

WITHOUT

REALLY

TRYING

☆☆☆　●●●　△△　F　M

**Zauberflöte, Die** (Mozart) (*The Magic Flute*) A mixed up story, but sublime music known to all. Production values must be high for full effect. Ger. (See also Page 72)

☆☆☆　●●●　△△△　F　N

**Zigeunerbaron, Der** (J. Strauss) (*The Gypsy Baron*) The closest a Strauss operetta ever comes to being an opera. Good story and nice music. Ger.

# *Index*

SEE ALSO *Quick Check List* beginning on Page 135, which alphabetically lists and describes most operas in the repertoire today. Index includes only references in the book itself.

**Bold** page numbers designate pictures
*Italic* page numbers designate entries of significance

Abbreviations:
(a) Artist, designer, etc.
(b) Book, play, literary work
(c) Composer
(d) Director, producer
(f) Film
(l) Librettist, author, etc.
(m) Manager, administrator
(o) Opera, operetta, musical
(p) Performer, actor, etc.
(s) Singer

HOW TO

ENJOY

OPERA

WITHOUT

REALLY

TRYING

HOW TO

ENJOY

OPERA

WITHOUT

REALLY

TRYING

HOW TO
ENJOY
OPERA
WITHOUT
REALLY
TRYING

# Acknowledgments

FA Fayer and Co GmbH 2,14,90
Elisabeth Hausmann 10,35
James Heffernan 17,47,94
Branco Gaica 28
Dominic Photography 44,61,66,68,79
David Parker 66
Anne Kirchbach 76